Teacher's 1A Guide

Apple Pie
Delta's Beginning ESL Program

Sadae Iwataki, Editor
Jean Owensby
Greta Kojima
Joanne Abing

REVISED EDITION

© 1993 by Delta Systems Co., Inc.
Revised Edition 1995

ISBN 0-937354-60-0

Delta Systems Co., Inc.
1400 Miller Parkway
McHenry, IL 60050 U.S.A.

Apple Pie 1A
Table of Contents

To the Teacher

Thank you for choosing Delta's **Apple Pie** as your ESL textbook. This series brings to you a comprehensive, carefully structured, realistically paced curriculum for the "beginning low" and "beginning high" levels, as defined by California's English as a Second Language Model Standards for Adult Education Programs, in four books: student book 1A and 1B for beginning low ESL and student books 2A and 2B for beginning high ESL. It is appropriate for adult and young adult learners in the United States and abroad. Its content and structure were developed over many years of use in the adult ESL programs of the Los Angeles Unified School District.

The following is a brief overview of the lesson structure of **Apple Pie**, and general directions for using the teaching notes in this guide.

Something New: Every lesson begins with this oral introduction of new material through use of visuals to accompany a listening comprehension selection. The target vocabulary and structures are introduced without the textbook through a series of steps: listen only, comprehension check, listen and repeat, listen and respond.

Let's Talk: This is a dialogue that incorporates the new language in the meaningful context of a dialogue set in a real–life situation. Students first master the dialogue orally with the help of a dialogue visual, then practice it with and without the teacher's help, and finally practice it with a partner and /or say it aloud from memory.

Practice, Interaction, Practice Activity: These are sections that expand on the language presented in the previous sections by using it again in mini–dialogues for pair practice, situations for role plays, group activities, and mixers. The practice sections move from more controlled oral work to more open–ended or personalized oral practice.

Reading: Reading passages are related to the lesson topic, using similar structures and vocabulary to present new information. They are followed by discussion questions, which generally end with a reference to students' own thoughts or experiences.

Writing: The writing sections provide review and reinforcement while giving students a chance to practice spelling and punctuation. In books 2A and 2B, some lessons have sections called *More Writing*, which provide prompts for controlled or original writing of sentences and short paragraphs.

After the core lesson, it is important to continue using the new language by including the *Review* and *Activity Pages* in subsequent class sessions. This way students have many opportunities to internalize new structures and functions and use them in their everyday interactions in English. The *Activity Pages* may include focused listening exercises, "information gap" activities, games, mixers, reading and discussion of true stories, and other tasks that integrate the language skills in a variety of relevant, interesting activities which provide student–student interaction and skill–building opportunities.

After each of the eight units of three related lessons, there is an **Evaluation**, with Listening Comprehension, Reading, and Writing sections. This regular evaluation is meant to be done individually and then corrected to give students an indication of their progress and teachers an indication of the current needs of the class.

An essential element in the pedagogy of **Apple Pie** is the use of the hand–held **visuals** available for each book. These contain the illustrations for the *Something New* and *Let's Talk* sections of the lessons, and are used to teach new vocabulary, structures, and functions with aural and visual cues for understanding. On the back of each visual are the phrases, sentences, or dialogue to be presented, to that the new language can be introduced as students listen without looking at the textbook.

The *Let's Talk* and *Reading* sections, focused listening sections of the *Activity Pages*, and Listening Comprehension sections of the *Evaluations* also appear on the **Apple Pie Cassette** available to accompany each book. Instructions are given in this teacher's guide for presenting those sections by using the cassette to provide opportunities for students to develop better listening skills by hearing different voices, by hearing new material before they read it, and by doing listening exercises that require them to glean information to carry out a task.

Guide to symbols used in the teacher's guide:

 The "closed book" symbol is a reminder that this is an oral section of the presentation, during which students are not yet looking at their books.

 This symbol means "now open your books" and indicates that students are about to see in print the items that they have been practicing orally.

 This group symbol indicates that students will be moving around the room in an interaction that requires them to speak to several students, or that they will be participating in a group activity.

 A cassette symbol in the heading means that a section is recorded on the tape, allowing an alternative presentation of the section by having students listen to a dialogue, listen while reading a passage, or listen and pick out specific information in a focused listening exercise.

At the beginning of each lesson in the teacher's guide, you will find Communication Objectives for the lesson, new structures that appear in the lesson, and a list of the visuals and other instructional aids needed for presenting the lesson to your class.

Good luck and success to you all. We hope that the **Apple Pie** program will serve you well, and that your students will find learning English our way to be effective, confidence–building and fun!

Hi! I'm Tony

Communication Objectives:
>Greet others in class
>Introduce oneself
>Ask for and give first and last name
>Spell first and last name
>Respond to simple classroom directions

Structures:
>Present of *be*
>Contractions *I'm, it's*
>Possessives *my, your*
>Imperatives
>Questions with *what*

Visuals:
>V1   Let's Talk: Hi! I'm Tony
>(also for Let's Talk: What's Your Last Name?)

Other instructional aids: 5" x 8" cards or heavy paper for name cards

Page 2
Something New: Classroom Directions

1. Briefly explain lesson objectives.

2. Say "Listen" and gesture for students to listen only as you repeat two or three times:
>Hello, class.
>Hello, students.
>My name's _____ .
>I'm _____ .

3. Say "Repeat" and gesture for the class to repeat:
>T: Hello, <u>(your name)</u> .
>Ss: Hello, <u>(your name)</u> .

4. Call on whole class, then individuals to repeat your name, then the phrase "Hello, _____ ."

5. Say "Answer" and gesture for the class to answer:

      T: Hello, class.
      Ss: Hello, <u>(your name)</u> .

6. Say "Answer" and gesture for individuals to answer:

      T: My name's _____ . What's your name?
      S1: <u>Maria Diaz</u> .
      S2: <u>Ken Wong</u> , etc.

7. Say "Answer" and gesture for individuals to answer:

      T: Hello, (student's name) .
      S: Hello, (your name) .

Page 3 **Let's Talk:** Hi! I'm Tony*

 1. Show the visual to establish the context of the conversation. Explain that Tony and May are students.

2. Model the dialogue as students listen, indicating the speakers by pointing to the visual or other means.

3. Model the dialogue again.

4. Model the dialogue and have class repeat.

5. Take one role and have class take other role; then change roles.

6. Divide class in half and have them take the two roles; then have them switch roles.

7. Have volunteers say the dialogue for the class.

 8. Have class open books and practice the dialogue in pairs.

*Cassette users can have students listen to the dialogue first with books closed.

☛ Practice: "Hi! I'm Tony"

 Have several rows (or groups) practice the two–part exchange, beginning with yourself and a student:

      T: Hi! I'm _____ .
      S1: Hi! I'm _____ .
Then S1 speaks to S2:
      S1: Hi! I'm _____ .
      S2: Hi! I'm _____ .
Then S2 continues the chain drill by speaking with S3, S3 with S4, S4 with S5, etc.

☛ Practice: "Nice to meet you"

Repeat the procedure for the chain drill in the practice above.

★ Something Extra

1. Note the variations given and have students repeat.

2. Ask volunteers to do a similar conversation for the class.

3. If the class can understand it, explain that "Nice to meet you" is an informal expression. "I'm happy to meet you" or "I'm glad to meet you" might be used in a more formal situation such as when meeting someone who's older or is an important person.

Page 4 **Let's Talk:** What's Your Last Name?*

1. Use V1 again or the illustration in the book to establish the context.

2. Follow the procedure given in the Let's Talk section above for presenting the dialogue.

 3. Have the students practice in pairs.

*Cassette users can have students listen to the dialogue first with books closed.

☛ Practice: "What's your first name?"

1. After the dialogue, continue the question and answer drill with a few students. Note any cultural characteristics of first and last names that may cause confusion. For example:

   (1) Spanish speakers sometimes use their mother's family name in combination with the father's; the mother's family name is placed after the father's, e.g., Tony Vega Garcia.

   (2) The Chinese, Japanese, and Koreans are used to giving last names first. They are somewhat formal in addressing each other and may feel hesitant about using first names freely.

2. Have students continue the question and answer pattern, or have them open their books and practice with a partner.

■ Interaction

 1. Have students walk around the room, introducing themselves to other students.

2. Have students carry on a conversation, exchanging first and last names.

3. Have them use the example as a guide.

Page 5 ## 🔘 Reading: The Alphabet*

1. Write the alphabet on the board or make a transparency of page 5.

2. Point out the difference between capital letters and small letters.

3. Have students listen as you read the alphabet.

4. Have students repeat the alphabet after you.

5. Have students read the alphabet aloud with you, working on the pronunciation of the letters.

*Cassette users can have the students listen to the alphabet on tape before they repeat the letters.

✍ Writing: The Alphabet

1. Have students follow the dotted lines and trace the letters of the alphabet.

2. Have students copy the alphabet.

Page 6 ## ☞ Practice: "Spell your name"

1. Place a few names on the chalkboard.

	First Name	Last Name
1.	*Lisa*	*Leiva*
2.		
3.		
4.		

2. Have students read the letters of their first and last names.

☞ Practice Activity: Print your name

1. Go over the directions and explain the meaning of *print*.

2. Have students write their own names first.

3. Pair students and ask them to ask and write down their partners' names.

☞ Practice Activity: Name cards

1. Prepare sheets of paper or 5" x 7" cards for students to make name cards for their desks.

2. Make a sample name card with your first and last name to demonstrate.

3. Have the students make their own name cards, following the directions in the text.

4. Call on students to show their cards and give their names.

5. Collect the cards at the end of class or ask students to keep the cards and bring to class every day.

Lesson 1 Activity Page

Page 7

A. Look!

Have students listen as you say the words and demonstrate on the board. Optional: Do a "dictation" with these three actions as the commands. (Students write letters, circles, etc.)

B. Read and do it!

1. Do #1, 2, and 3 with the class, demonstrating on the board.

2. Correct the first three items; then have students continue independently.

3. Correct as a class.

Touch the Floor

Communication Objectives:
> Identify classroom objects
> Follow simple directions
> Introduce others

New Structures:
> *This is...* for introductions

Visuals:
> V2   Let's Talk: This Is My Friend Sara

Page 8   ✔ **Review**

1. Name cards: Have volunteers show their name cards and read their names, giving the first and last names. Have them spell their names out loud.

2. The alphabet: Reproduce the exercise on the board or a transparency. Have volunteers match the capital and small letters.

Page 9   **Something New:** Classroom Objects

1. Briefly explain lesson objectives.

2. Have students listen as you hold up or point to an object and identify it. Say:

a pencil	It's a pencil.
a door	It's a door.

3. Have the class repeat the words after you.

4. Write the names of the items on the board, or show a transparency of the classroom objects section of page 9.

5. Read the names of the objects as the class listens.

6. Have the class read the words after you.

☞ **Practice: "It's a window"**

1. Use classroom objects (walk up to the chalkboard, windows, or door), or the overhead projector and have students respond as a class, groups, and individuals:
    T: What's this?
    S: It's a window. (door, etc.)

2. Then have students ask each other.

Something New: Following Directions

1. Have students listen and watch as you touch the following items and name them:
    chair   desk   floor   book   pen

2. Have students touch the items as you call out the names. Say, for example:
    Touch a chair.

3. Model the words and have students repeat as they touch the items.

4. Have students listen and watch as you hold up and put down the following items and name them:
    pen   pencil   book   notebook

5. Have students hold up, then put down, the items as you call out the names.

6. Model the words and have students repeat as they hold up and put down each item.

7. Have students listen and watch as you point to the following items and name them:
    chalkboard   windows   door
    clock   wall   flag

8. Have students point to the items as you call out the names. Say:
    Point to a window.

9. Model the words and have students repeat as they point to the items.

10. Have students hold up and put down, touch, or point to an object as you say: Show me a…

Page 10   ☞ **Practice Activity: Point to the flag**

1. Use classroom objects or the transparency to give directions: point to, touch, hold up, etc.

2. Have students respond appropriately as a class and individually.

 3. Have pairs or groups of students take turns giving directions to each other, as their classmates respond to the directions.

Let's Talk: This Is My Friend Sara*

1. Introduce two students to each other to establish a context and set the pattern.
   Teacher: *Yolanda*, this is *Al*.
   Al, this is *Yolanda*.

   [Cue the students' responses.]

   Yolanda: Nice to meet you, Al.
   Al: Nice to meet you, Yolanda.

2. Show V2–1A to establish the context of the dialogue. Explain that this is the second day of school and May has brought a friend to class. She is introducing her to Mrs. Baker.

3. Model the dialogue twice.

4. Follow these steps for presenting the dialogue:
   a. Have groups, then individuals, repeat lines. Take roles with the students.
   b. Have groups, then individuals, take roles.
   c. Write the dialogue on the board or show it on the overhead.
   d. Read the lines.
   e. Have class, groups, then individuals, read the lines after you.

 5. Have class open books and practice the dialogue in triads.

*Cassette users can have students listen to the dialogue first with books closed.

Page 11   ☛ **Practice: "This is my friend"**

1. Have students form groups of three.

2. Have members of each group practice introducing each other.
   [NOTE: Point out to students that "How do you do?" is an expression that is often used when one is being introduced. Point out also that the response is "How do you do?" and not "Fine, thank you."]

☛ Practice Activity: Meeting other students

1. Have four volunteers come to the front of the room, holding their name cards.

2. Introduce the volunteers to the class.

3. Have the remaining students form pairs. (Make sure that they know each other's names.)

4. Have pairs come up in turn to introduce their partners to the volunteers in front or to the whole class.

Reading: A New Student*

1. Explain the concept of middle names.

2. Have the students read the selection silently.

3. Have volunteers read the selection aloud.

4. Facilitate a discussion on middle names.

5. Explain the *yes* or *no* activity and have the class complete it.

*Cassette users can have students listen to the Reading first with books closed.

✍ Writing: The Alphabet (Cursive)

Page 12

1. Show transparency or write the alphabet (cursive) on the board.

2. If students' literacy levels are high enough, have them copy the letters from the textbook, board, or transparency.

3. Show examples and contrast printing and cursive writing.

4. Have the students print their names.

5. Have the students sign their names.

Lesson 2 Activity Pages

Page 13 📼 *A. Listen to the spelling. Write the name.**

1. Go over the directions.

2. Play the tape or use the script to read number 1. Check to see that students understand what to do. Continue with numbers 2–6. Pause between items if necessary to allow time to write.

Script:
Listen to the spelling. Write the names. Number one is an example. Listen and look at the example.

1. This is Eliza.
   E–L–I–Z–A?
   Yes, Eliza.

2. This is Chris.
   C–H–R–I–S?
   Yes, Chris.

3. This is Henry.
   H–E–N–R–Y?
   Yes, Henry.

4. This is Vera.
   V–E–R–A?
   Yes, Vera.

5. This is John.
   J–O–H–N?
   Yes, John.

6. This is Gina.
   G–I–N–A?
   Yes, Gina.

3. Have volunteers write the answers on the board.

4. Correct by having students compare their answers to those on the board.

5. (Optional) Practice spelling the names aloud.

*Cassette users can have students listen to the script on tape.

B. Look and read.

Have students work in the book; then have volunteers do the same on the board to check.

C. Write.

Have students read each instruction and write. Circulate around the room to check.

Page 14

D. Listen and write.

1. Explain that students will listen and write the spelling of each word.

2. Use the script to read each item.

> **Script:**
> Listen and write the word.
>
> 1. It's a chair, C–H–A–I–R.
>
> 2. It's a notebook, N–O–T–E–B–O–O–K.
>
> 3. It's a pencil, P–E–N–C–I–L.
>
> 4. It's a clock, C–L–O–C–K.
>
> 5. It's a window, W–I–N–D–O–W.
>
> 6. It's a door, D–O–O–R.

Page 15

E. Say the word. Spell the word. Circle the picture. Write the word.

1. Do number 1 together as an example.

2. Have students read each word aloud, read the spelling aloud, choose the correct picture, and write the word. (The whole class can work together or pairs or individuals can do this.) Have students do every step, as this is a memorizing task.

How Are You Today?

Communication Objectives:
> Greet others
> Respond to the greeting *How are you?*
> Say *goodbye*

New Structures:
> Adverbs *later, tomorrow*

Visuals:
> V3   fine
> V4   okay
> V5   Let's Talk: Bye, Tony

Page 16

✔ Review

1. The cursive alphabet: Copy the exercise on the board or show on transparency. Have volunteers write in the missing letters.

2. Following directions: Have class, groups, and individuals follow your directions to touch, point to, hold up, or put down classroom objects.

Page 17

Something New: How Are You today?

1. Have students listen and watch as you ask, "How are you today?"

2. Show V3 and respond, "I'm fine, thank you."

3. Show V3 and have students repeat, "I'm fine, thank you."

4. Ask, "How are you today?" Show V3 and have students respond, "I'm fine, thank you."

5. Repeat above steps with V4.

Let's Talk: I'm Fine, Thanks*

1. Show the visual to establish the context of the conversation. Say:
   Tony sees May and greets her.

2. Model the dialogue as students listen, indicating the speakers by pointing to the visual or other means.

3. Model the dialogue again.

4. Model the dialogue and have class repeat.

5. Take one role and have class take other role; then change roles.

6. Divide class in half and have them take the two roles; then have them switch roles.

7. Have volunteers say the dialogue for the class.

 8. Have class open books and practice the dialogue and the following Practice: "I'm fine" in pairs.

*Cassette users can have students listen to the dialogue first with books closed.

Page 18 ## ■ Interaction: Hi Sara, How Are You?

 1. Have students move around the room, greeting four people and asking how they feel.

2. Tell them to say how they actually feel, fine or okay.

Let's Talk: Bye, Tony*

1. Show V5 to establish the context of the conversation.

2. Follow the procedure given in the Let's Talk section above for presenting the dialogue.

 3. Have the students practice in pairs.

*Cassette users can have students listen to the dialogue first with books closed.

★ Something Extra: Saying Goodbye

1. Elicit and present the various expressions used for leave–taking.

2. Discuss and practice both formal and informal expressions, establishing the proper contexts: e.g., to a teacher, to a peer, to an older person, to a child, etc.

☛ Practice: "So long, Maria"

Have several students practice various ways of saying goodbye to others by establishing various contexts for them:
Say goodbye to: a good friend
a small child
the principal
etc.
You can also ask rows or groups of students to come up with the appropriate phrases.

Page 19 ## ■ Interaction: Hello and Goodbye

Have students go around the room, practicing greetings and leave–takings.

🖭 Reading: Greetings*

1. Have the students read the selection silently.

2. Have the class read the selection aloud.

3. Ask for volunteers to read the sentences aloud.

4. Facilitate a discussion on how they usually greet and leave friends and family.

*Cassette users can have students listen to the tape before opening their books and/or listen as they read the passage silently.

✍ Writing

1. Go over the directions with the class and have them complete the exercise.

2. Have pairs correct the exercise by reading it together as a dialogue.

Delta's Apple Pie, Teacher's Guide 1A

Lesson 3 Activity Pages

Page 20

A. Read and write.

Give the directions: Students will select a word from the box for each blank. Point to the pictures to show who's speaking in each line.

Page 21

B. Copy the letters.

Demonstrate by writing a few students' names on the board in cursive. Have students practice the cursive alphabet by copying the letters in their notebooks. Skip this exercise if your students' level of literacy doesn't allow them to switch to cursive comfortably.

Page 22

C. Read, copy, and do it.

1. Have students read and copy each sentence. (You can have them copy in block letters or in cursive as appropriate.)

2. Ask pairs to read the instructions to each other; partners demonstrate the actions.

Unit One  **Evaluation**

Page 23

Sample Exercise

1. Explain to the students that every third lesson in the book will contain an Evaluation to see what they have learned and what they may need to review.

2. Have students turn to the Evaluation Sample Exercise in their books.

3. Reproduce the Sample Exercise on the board or overhead and provide practice in the use of:
   correct/incorrect
   right/wrong
   circle
   choose

4. Have students complete the Sample Exercise.

5. Go over the correct answers as a class.

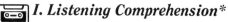 ***I. Listening Comprehension****

　　　　1. Now have students turn to page 24 for the first part of the evaluation.

　　　　2. Read each item of the script two times, at normal conversational speed.

　　　　　　　Script:
　　　　　　　1. Spell your name.

　　　　　　　2. What's your last name?

　　　　　　　3. Touch the chair.

　　　　　　　4. Hold up the book.

　　　　　　　5. So long.

　　　　　　　6. Print your name.

　　　　*Cassette users can have students listen to the script on the tape.

　　II. Reading and III. Writing

　　　　1. Go over the directions for Parts II and III with students.

　　　　2. Have class do these sections independently.

Evaluation Check

　　　　1. Correct evaluation by having student volunteers write their answers on the board or an overhead transparency.

　　　　2. Have class check their answers.

　　　　3. Circulate to make sure students have checked their work accurately.

Lesson 4

What's Your Address?

Communication Objectives:
Ask for and give personal information
Spell and say numbers aloud
Keep an address book

New Structures:
None

Visuals:
V6   Let's Talk: What's Your Address?
V7   registration form

Other instructional aids:
Suggested realia—School registration form
Address book
United States map
Envelope

Page 28

✔ Review: Our Classroom

1. Review the classroom objects learned in the previous lessons.

2. Present objects again, this time counting the number:
   Pencils: one, two, three pencils
   Chairs: etc.

3. Have students suggest other items to count.

Page 29

Something New: Numbers

1. Have students listen as you hold up a finger and say "one." Repeat "one." Continue with numbers 2 through 12. Hold up various numbers of fingers and say the numbers.

2. Have students hold up the correct number of fingers as you give command. (Say numbers in sequence, then say numbers at random.)

3. Hold up finger and say "one," having class repeat. Continue with numbers 2 through 12, having class repeat. Hold up various numbers of fingers at random, having class repeat.

4. Cue with fingers; have class, groups, and individuals call out the numbers.

5. Write the numbers on board as you say them, having class repeat.

6. Write numbers in order and at random; have class, groups, individuals say them.

 Let's Talk: What's Your Address?*

1. Hold up V7 or a registration form from your school and identify it. Draw a similar form on the board or show one on the overhead projector. (You can use your school registration form or the form on page 35 in the student book.)

2. Write in personal information for yourself, telling the class:
   My name is…
   My address is…
   My city is…

3. Show V6 to establish the context of the conversation. Point to the persons in the visual. Say:
   This is Ben Lee. He is at Westside Adult School. He is in the office. This is the school clerk. She is helping him with the registration form.

4. Model the dialogue as students listen, indicating the speakers by pointing to them as you speak.

5. Model the dialogue again. Point out that the number 104 is pronounced "one oh four." You might want to write only the numbers (104, 90018, 555–6370) on the board to help students memorize the dialogue.

6. Model the dialogue and have class repeat.

7. Take one role and have class take other role; then change roles.

8. Divide class in half and have them take the two roles; then have them switch roles.

9. Have volunteers say the dialogue for the class.

10. Have class open books and practice the dialogue in pairs.

   *Cassette users can have students listen to the dialogue first with books closed.

☛ **Practice: "My address is 109 Union Avenue"**

1. Tell the class your address and then ask several students their addresses.

2. Tell the class your city and then ask several students their cities.

3. Continue with the other information on the registration form pictured.

4. Have students open their books and read the exercise in pairs.

★ **Something Extra:** Area Codes for Telephones

1. Establish the context of calling long distance by asking class if they know people in other cities. Ask if they call these people on the phone and how they dial those numbers.

2. Write the area codes for the cities in the book and those that the students tell you on the board.

3. Explain how to call someone in one of those cities:
   Call a friend in Chicago. The number is 322–6571.
   Dial 1, then dial the area code, then the number.
   Dial 1 + 312 + 322–6571.

4. Go over the process with other cities, and other telephone numbers (elicited from the students, if possible).

5. Have students open their books and read the information.

6. Have them complete the exercise of writing in the digits to dial for the phone numbers in the cities listed. (Fill in the last blanks with cities that are familiar to class and are in another phone area.)

Something New: State Abbreviations

1. Put up a wall map of the U.S., if available, or have class open their books to the map in book.

2. Point out the state your class is in and other familiar states: California, Illinois, Texas, Florida, New York, etc.

3. Write the postal abbreviations for these states on the board, and have class read the abbreviations. Ask: "What is the abbreviation for California?" etc. Have class read the letters.

4. Using the map in the book, have class draw a line from the abbreviations to the appropriate states.

5. If your state is not shaded, have class write in the abbreviation for their state.

■ Interaction: Address Book

1. Show a real address book, if available. (Someone in the class may have one.) Indicate how people write friends' names and addresses in the book.

2. Show some examples of pages from an address book on the board: R page with a Mr. Reeves, M page with a Mrs. Martin, etc.

3. Tell students that they need to ask to get names and addresses of their classmates in the "address books" and have them practice: "Please write your name and address (in my address book)." Teach them an appropriate response: "Okay." "All right." etc.

4. Have them walk around the room getting names and addresses of at least two other students in the book. Monitor activity to encourage students to give the request in English.

Page 33

★ Something Extra: Commas

1. Have the class read the information with you to prepare for the Practice Activity below.

2. Elicit the cities and state of the students in the class and write them on the board.

☛ Practice Activity: A letter to a friend

1. Show an addressed envelope. Explain the position of the return address and the address of the person being sent the letter. Point out the stamp location.

2. Have class look at the envelope in the book. Show the return address position and have them write their return address.

3. Ask students to address the envelope to a friend or relative.

4. Point out the use of the state abbreviations on the envelope.

Page 34

🔊 Reading: Ruben's Letter to a Friend*

1. Have class look at the picture and tell what they see in the picture.

2. Have class read the story silently.

3. Ask comprehension questions:

       Is Ruben's city Los Angeles?

       Is Lan Yee's city Los Angeles?

       What is Lan Yee's zip code? etc.

4. Read the story out loud and have students read silently.

5. Have class read passage together.

*Cassette users can have students listen to the Reading first with books closed, then listen as they read along.

✍ Writing

1. Have class do Writing activity independently, circulating to help as needed.

2. Correct activity together.

Lesson 4 Activity Page

Page 35 *A. Listen and write the missing information.**

1. Explain that students will hear someone talking, and they must try to hear the numbers needed to fill in the blanks. (This is a focused listening exercise, and so there should not be pauses between the items. The task is to discern the missing information while listening to natural speech.)

2. Play the tape or read the whole script as many times as necessary for students to fill in the blanks.

       Script:

       1. My name is Paul Smith. My address is 312 Pine Street, Houston, Texas. My zip code is 77099.

       2. My name is Yuki Ohara. My address is 746 Grand Avenue, Los Angeles, California. My zip code is 90012.

       3. My name is Sunay Kim. My address is 592 5th Avenue, New York, New York. My zip code is 10016.

       4. My name is Henry Lee. My address is 813 Elm Boulevard, Seattle, Washington. My zip code is 98103.

*Cassette users can have students listen to the script on tape.

B. Read and do it.

    1. Have students read and answer in writing without oral instructions.

    2. Circulate to check.

C. Read the directions. Fill in the form.

    1. Go over the directions.

    2. Go through the vocabulary items on the form, pointing to each one and saying it as the students read.

    3. Have students fill in the form.

    4. Circulate to correct and/or have volunteers fill in their forms on an overhead transparency. (Note: you can also copy this page and have students turn in their work.)

What Time Is It?

Communication Objectives:
Ask for and give the time
Use *Excuse me* to get attention
Use *Thank you* and *You're welcome*
Use appropriate greetings

New Structures:
None

Visuals:

V8	Let's Talk: What Time Is It?
V9	morning
V10	afternoon
V11	evening

Other instructional aids: Cardboard clock face with movable hands, if available

Page 36

✔ Review: Numbers

 1. Dictate the sentences. Have students fill in the numbers in their books.

Script:
1. My address is 610 Fletcher Drive.
2. He has six books.
3. She has four pencils.
4. There are eleven windows in the room.
5. My zip code is 60050.
6. My address is 1203 Rush Street.
7. The school telephone number is 682–7415.

2. Correct the numbers as a class.

Something New: Telling Time

 1. Briefly explain the objectives of the lesson.

2. Hold up a cardboard clock or draw a picture of a clock on the board. Move the hands as you call out the time: 1 o'clock to 12 o'clock.

3. Set the time, say it, and get a *yes/no* response from class.

4. Practice responses: *"Yes, it is/No, it isn't."* Ask: Is it_____? and have class, groups, individuals respond appropriately.

5. Set time. Ask: "What time is it?" and have class, groups, individuals answer.

Page 37 **Let's Talk:** What Time Is It?*

1. Show V8 to establish the situation. Say:
   Sara is at the bus stop. She doesn't have her watch. Mrs. Green is at the bus stop too. She has her watch.

2. Model the dialogue as students listen, indicating the speakers by pointing to the visual or other means.

3. Model the dialogue again.

4. Model the dialogue and have class repeat.

5. Take one role and have class take other role; then change roles.

6. Divide class in half and have them take the two roles; then have them switch roles.

7. Have volunteers say the dialogue for the class.

 8. Have class open books and practice the dialogue in pairs.

*Cassette users can have students listen to the dialogue first with books closed.

☛ **Practice: "What time is it?"**

1. Using the cardboard clock or clocks drawn on board, practice giving a polite interruption and asking the time with different times, as a class, in groups and pairs.

2. Have class practice with a partner what they have been doing orally.

Page 38 **Something New:** Greetings

 1. On the board depict a day by showing the progress of the sun from morning to sunset; then show stars and a moon. Stand by the appropriate part of the day to model the greetings: Good morning, Good afternoon, and Good evening.

2. Show visuals and model the greetings again.

3. Show visuals and model a greeting; have class repeat.

4. Show visuals and have class, groups, individuals give the appropriate greetings to classmate; have classmate respond.

Extension Activity

1. Teach the terms "a.m." and "p.m." by using the time of day visuals: e.g., morning visual as 6 a.m. or 8 a.m.; afternoon and evening visual as 5 p.m., 8 p.m.

2. Explain 12 o'clock as "noon" and "midnight."

☞ Practice: "It's 10 o'clock"

1. Show greeting visuals V9–11 with a clock to combine greeting with time question. Have class respond appropriately.

 2. Have class open their books and practice with partners.

Page 39 ## Something New: It's 1:30

 1. Show the time (with cardboard clock or on the board) and model half–hour times, 1:30 to 12:30.

2. Check for comprehension.

3. Ask: "What time is it?" showing various half–hours on board or on cardboard clock for class, groups, individuals to answer.

4. Alternate hour and half–hour times for further practice.

☞ Practice: "It's 3:30"

 Have class practice in pairs what they have been practicing orally.

📼 Reading: Good Morning, Ben*

1. Have class look at the picture and identify the people.

2. Have class read the selection independently.

3. Ask comprehension questions about reading: Does Mr. Green want to know about the bus? Is Bob Lewis or Ben Tran the person with a watch? What do you say when you don't know something?

*Cassette users can have students listen to the Reading first with books closed.

☞ **Practice: "I'm sorry. I don't know"**

1. Model the expression "I'm sorry. I don't know."

2. Have class repeat the expression.

3. Ask: "What time is it?" and have class respond.

4. Vary response with some students who know the time, some who don't. Indicate that some people have watches, some don't, and have them respond appropriately.

 5. Have students open their books and practice with a partner.

✑ Writing

1. Have students do Writing independently.

2. Correct the activity as a class.

Lesson 5 Activity Pages

📼 ***A. Listen. Circle the correct letter.****

1. Explain that students will listen and choose one of the times given by circling the letter, a, b, or c. Use number 1 as an example.

2. Play the tape or use the script to read the items as many times as necessary.

3. Correct as a class.

> **Script:**
> 1. It's 5:00.   Let's go home.
>
> 2. It's 6:30.   Let's eat.
>
> 3. It's 12:00.   Let's have lunch.
>
> 4. It's 3:30.   Let's take a break.
>
> 5. It's 7:30.   Let's go to a movie.
>
> 6. It's 9:30.   Let's watch t.v.

*Cassette users can have students listen to the script on tape.

B. Read the time. Draw the hands on the clock.

    1. Go over directions and have students do the exercise on their own.

    2. Correct by having pairs compare their work, or by drawing the correct answers on the board or a transparency.

Page 42   ***C. Look at the picture and write the greeting.***

    1. Optional: Review greetings with visuals V9–11 from Lesson 5 for *morning*, *afternoon*, and *evening*.

    2. Have individuals, pairs, or groups decide on appropriate greetings and write them in.

Page 43   ***D. Work with a partner.***

    1. Explain the word *opinion*. You might want to teach "I think it's_____."

    2. Have pairs discuss the pictures and write down what time they think it is in each picture.

I'm Sorry I'm Late

Communication Objectives:
Apologize for being late
Respond to an apology
Use *Good night* for leavetaking

New Structures:
Yes/No questions
Short answers *Yes, it is/No, it isn't*
Adjectives *early, late*

Visuals:
V9   morning (from Lesson 5)
V10   afternoon (from Lesson 5)
V11   evening (from Lesson 5)
V12   It's early
V13   It's late
V14   Let's Talk: I'm Sorry I'm Late (Sara and custodian)
V15   Let's Talk: I'm Sorry I'm Late (Sara and Mrs. Baker)

Page 44

✔ Review: Time

Have students work in small groups with a movable clock or cards with different times written on them.

S1: What time is it?
S2: It's _____ o'clock.
S3: What time is it? etc.

Something New: It's Early

1. Show V12 and discuss: Is this room empty or full? etc.

2. Indicate that class has not started yet: It is early.

3. Contrast V13 with V12 and discuss the differences.

4. Indicate the starting time of the class and the current time: It's late.

5. Use other examples if needed to establish the idea of early and late: e.g., appointments, bus schedules, etc.

Page 45 **Let's Talk:** I'm Sorry I'm Late*

1. Show V14 and establish the situation: Point out the ongoing English class and the student who has just arrived, who is outside the classroom. She knows she is late and is asking the custodian about the time.

2. Show V15 and establish the situation: The student is apologizing to the teacher for being late.

3. Model the dialogue as students listen, indicating the speakers by pointing to the visual or other means.

4. Model the dialogue again.

5. Model the dialogue and have class repeat.

6. Take one role and have class take other role; then change roles.

7. Divide class in half and have them take the two roles; then have them switch roles.

8. Have class open books and practice the dialogue and the following Practice: "I'm early" in pairs. (Note that the Practice continues on page 46, #3–4.)

*Cassette users can have students listen to the dialogue first with books closed.

Page 46 ☛ **Practice: "That's okay"**

1. Ask questions to elicit from students a description of each situation pictured:
   Where is he/she?
   What's wrong?
   What time is it? etc.

2. Elicit from whole class what should go in the blanks; then have them fill in the missing words.

Page 47 **Reading:** Kim Is Early; Bob Is Late*

1. Before reading, have students look at the pictures. Ask comprehension questions to establish the situation of people coming to a party.

2. Have class read the passage silently.

3. Have them respond to the *yes/no* statements.

4. Ask questions about the reading, asking *yes/no, either/or,* and *wh—* questions.

5. Ask departure questions using the topic of being early or late to parties:
> Do you go to parties early or late?
> When you have a party at your house, do you want people to be early or late?
> What do you do with people who come early?
> Do you think it is good to be early?
> Is it more important to be early for work or for appointments?

Students may be more able to answer *yes/no* or *either/or* questions. You may need to interpret and make statements for what students are trying to say.

*Cassette users can have students listen to the Reading first.

Let's Talk: Good Night, Kim*

1. Have class look at the illustration of this activity to establish the situation: It is late, and people are starting to go home.

2. Have students close their books and practice the dialogue in groups of three.

3. Point out that "Good evening" is a greeting, and "Good night" is a goodbye.

*Cassette users can have students listen to the dialogue first with books closed.

Page 48
☛ Practice: "Good evening, Tony"

1. Using visuals of morning, afternoon, and night (V9–11), cue students and have them give appropriate greetings and leave–takings.

2. Have students practice in pairs, using partners' real names.

Page 49
✐ Writing

1. Have students fill in the missing words to complete the exchanges.

2. Correct Writing exercise as a class.

Page 50

A. Talk about the picture.

Have whole class, group, or pairs discuss the picture.

B. Look at the picture. Read the questions and circle the answers.

1. Have individuals do the exercise.

2. Correct as a class.

Page 51

C. Read the story. Write the missing words.

1. Lead a discussion about the picture.

2. Point out that the word box contains the answers to choose from. Have students fill in the blanks independently.

3. Correct as a class.

Unit Two  Evaluation

Page 53 **I. Listening Comprehension***

1. Go over the directions for Part I with students.

2. Read each item of the script two times, at normal conversational speed.

Script:

1. It's one o'clock.

2. It's 8 o'clock.

3. It's 8:30.

4. Is it 6:30?

5. Good morning.

6. Good evening.

7. My address is 306 Main Street.

8. My zip code is 90043.

*Cassette users can have students listen to the script on the tape.

II. Reading and III. Writing

    1. Go over the directions for Parts II and III with students.

    2. Have class do these sections independently.

Evaluation Check

    1. Correct evaluation by having student volunteers write their answers on the board or an overhead transparency.

    2. Have class check their answers.

    3. Circulate to make sure students have checked their work accurately.

I'm a Doctor; She's a Doctor, Too

Communication Objectives:
Identify occupations
Talk about one's occupation

New Structures:
Contractions *you're*, *he's*, *she's*
Short answers *Yes, he/she is/No, he/she isn't*

Visuals:
V16	a doctor
V17	a doctor
V18	a nurse
V19	a dishwasher
V20	a waiter
V21	a cook
V22	a secretary
V23	a homemaker
V24	a salesclerk
V25	a factory worker
V26	a bus driver
V27	a gardener
V28	Let's Talk: He's a Doctor, Too

Other instructional aids:
Cardboard clock face with movable hands, if available

Optional realia—Movie ad, TV schedule, party invitation (can be hand–made quickly), class schedule or registration slip

Page 56

✔ Review: It's Early/Late

1. Establish situations using movie ad, TV guide, etc., in turn.

2. Write on board "Movie" and "7 o'clock."
Ask/elicit response:
What time is the movie?
7 o'clock.

3. Also write "now" and the time now on the board.
   Ask/elicit response:

       What time is it now?

       It's _____ .

4. Have class make judgment if it is early or late for the activity.

 5. After practicing each item, have class open books.

6. Read together, then have students practice in pairs.

7. Students can then fill in the information in their books.

Page 57

Something New: Occupations

 1. Briefly state objective of the lesson.

2. Introduce concept of occupations and pronouns. Use self and several students as examples.

       T: I'm a teacher. You're a student. (Use gestures)

       S: I'm a student. You're a teacher. (Have students use gestures)

       T: He/She's a student. (Use gestures)

       T: What is he/she? (Have students respond appropriately)

3. Show visuals V16–27. Model statements with he and she.

       T: She's a doctor.

4. Check student comprehension.

   a. Show visuals and ask students to identify various occupations.

       T: Point to the homemaker, etc.

       Ss: She's a homemaker.

   b. Ask yes/no questions.

       T: Is he/she a doctor, busser, etc.?

       Ss: Yes/No

5. Show visuals. Model statements. Have class, groups, individual students repeat.

6. Show visuals. Ask: What is he/she? Have class, groups, individuals answer.

Page 58 **Let's Talk:** He's a Doctor, Too*

1. Show V28 and establish the situation. Say:

       Sara is at the hospital. Her husband Tomas is sick.

       There are many workers at the hospital.

   Ask questions about the situation to check for understanding.

2. Model the dialogue as students listen, indicating the speakers by pointing to the visual or other means.

3. Model the dialogue again.

4. Model the dialogue and have class repeat.

5. Take one role and have class take other role; then change roles.

6. Divide class in half and have them take the two roles; then have them switch roles.

7. Have volunteers say the dialogue for the class.

 8. Have class open books and practice the dialogue in pairs.

*Cassette users can have students listen to the dialogue first with books closed.

Page 59 ☛ **Practice: "Are you a student?"**

 1. Use substitution drills for student practice.
For example:

T: She's a	homemaker	Ss: She's a homemaker.
	salesclerk	She's a salesclerk.
	doctor	She's a doctor
	truck driver	She's a truck driver.
He		He's a truck driver.
	gardener	He's a gardener.
	student	He's a student.
	nurse	He's a nurse.
She		She's a nurse.
I		I'm a nurse.
You		You're a nurse.
	teacher	You're a teacher.

2. Use visuals to practice affirmative and negative sentences and Yes/No questions with he and she.

3. Give visuals to persons in class so that class can practice using names as well as pronouns. "Is Maria a doctor?"

 4. Have class open books and read what they have been practicing orally. Practice as class and in pairs.

☛ **Practice Activity: Talk about your job**

1. Have class break into small groups.

2. Have them practice using pronouns I, You, He, She, talking about their real occupations: e.g., I'm a homemaker. You're a busser. He's a waiter, etc. [Note: for occupations not in lesson, try to simplify the job titles. Use generic terms such as "office worker."]

3. Encourage the use of gestures for *I, you, he/she* to denote understanding.

4. Have a few students report back to class on what they learned about other students' occupations.

Reading: The English Teacher*

1. Have class read independently.

2. Ask yes/no, either/or, and then wh– questions to check comprehension.

3. Depart from story to ask students questions about their class, teacher, room number, etc.

4. Have class read the story aloud, as a whole class and then in pairs to each other.

5. Have class read and answer questions (phrases or one–word answers are all that are required) as a class and in paired practice.

*Cassette users can have students listen to the Reading first with books closed, then listen again and read along silently.

✐ **Writing**

[Note that there are six items on pages 60–61]

1. Have students write independently. If you notice that many are having problems, go over each item with the whole group first.

2. After class finishes Writing, go over each item and correct it together.

★ **Something Extra:** Your Occupation

Students who finish the Writing above quickly can be encouraged to write at least two sentences:

e.g., My name is _____ . I am a _____ .

Page 62   **A. Write the word, copy it and circle the picture.**

       1. Go over #1 as an example. Then check to see that students know what to do for #2.

       2. Have students do the exercise independently.

       3. Go over the answers by writing the words on the board and reviewing their spelling aloud.

Page 63   **B. Write.**

       1. Go over the picture and the sentence for #1.

       2. Have students do the exercise individually or in pairs.

| **Lesson 8**

Are You New Students?

Communication Objective:
Ask about occupations to socialize

New Structures:
Plurals
Short answers *Yes, they are/No, they aren't*

Visuals:

V29	student, students
V30	baker, bakers
V31	teacher, teachers
V32	gardener, gardeners
V33	lawyer, lawyers
V34	waiter, waiters
V35	barber, barbers
V36	dentist, dentists
V37	Let's Talk: Are You New Students?

Page 64

✔ Review: Occupations

1. Use visuals from Lesson 7 to review occupations. Have class open book and read the names of the occupations.

2. Have students draw line from written name of occupation to the places where they work.
[Note: Students can work individually or in groups.]

3. Correct sheet as a group. (Suggestion: Make a transparency of page and go over lesson with class, drawing in lines or having student volunteers do it.)

Page 65

Something New: People and Occupations

1. Show singular side of V29–36 and model:
   He's a student, etc.

2. Test for comprehension—Ask yes/no, then either/or questions about the various occupations, e.g., "Is he a barber?" "Is he a barber or a dentist?"

3. Have students repeat the names of each occupation.

4. Ask: "What is he/she?" and have class, groups, students answer.

5. Follow the same procedure for introducing the plural forms.

6. Vary the number—sometimes singular, sometimes plural—for practice.

7. Give the visuals to students who will assume role of pictured occupation. (Sometimes students can share a visual to indicate plural.) Practice with "Are you…?" and "I/We…" as well as "He/She/They…"

Page 66   ☞ **Practice: "Are they bakers?"**

1. Use the visuals to practice yes/no questions and answers.

 2. Have students open their books and read what they have been practicing orally, first as a class and then in pairs.

 Let's Talk: Are You New Students?*

1. Show V37 to establish the situation. Ask questions to check for comprehension of the situation.

2. Model the dialogue as students listen, indicating the speakers by pointing to the visual or other means.

3. Model the dialogue again.

4. Model the dialogue and have class repeat.

5. Divide class in three groups and have them take the three roles; then have them switch roles.

6. Have three volunteers say the dialogue for the class.

 7. Have class open books and practice the dialogue in triads.

*Cassette users can have students listen to the dialogue first with books closed.

Page 67   ☞ **Practice: "Are they barbers?"**

 1. Use real students and yourself and other teachers in school to ask singular and plural questions about students, teachers:
Are Mr. Smith and I teachers?
Jose, are you and Thanh students? etc.

2. Use the visuals to reinforce the singular and plural forms of pronouns and nouns. (Give the visuals to students to practice questions with "you"—one student for singular you/I, several students for plural you/we.

3. Be sure to give students opportunity to practice questions as well as answers.

4. After extensive oral practice, have students open their books and read the drills they have been practicing as a class and then in pairs.

☞ Practice: "Contractions"

1. Go over the sentences to review contractions and practice their pronunciation.

2. If necessary, review how the contractions are formed on the board. For practice, do the extension activity.

Extension Activity

To prepare for this activity, write each word of the uncontracted sentences in the Practice on large index cards. On the back of the cards for *am*, *is*, and *are*, write the alternative *'m*, *'s*, or *'re*.

1. Give one card for each word of a sentence to a group of students and have them go to the front of the room, arrange themselves in the order of the sentence, and show their cards to the class.

2. Have the whole class read the sentence aloud in its uncontracted form.

3. With the group still standing in line, ask the person with the *am/is/are* card to turn it over to reveal the contracted form. Then have him or her stand even closer to the person with the pronoun card and overlap their cards to form the contraction.

4. Have the whole class read the sentence aloud.

5. Continue with all the sentences, first uncontracted and then with contractions.

Page 68 ## ☞ Practice Activity: What's your job?

1. Have groups of four students talk to each other and give each other information about their real occupations.

2. In each group have each student give his/her occupation.

3. The others should listen and be able to understand and repeat each person's occupation in the group.

4. If there are two or more persons with the same occupation in the group, students can practice the plural forms of pronouns and nouns.

5. Have representative groups report to the class about occupations of people in their group.

6. Take a poll of what seems to be a popular occupation and talk about it: e.g., "In this class, Victor, Luisa, and Makoto are restaurant workers. Luisa and Victor are cooks. Makoto is a waiter."

📼 Reading: Adult School Students*

1. Explain what a busser does. (The term busser, rather than busboy, is used by food service employers.

2. Have class read the story by themselves first; then ask comprehension questions about the story.

3. Then read story together as a class, in groups or in pairs.

*Cassette users can have students listen to the Reading first with books closed.

Page 69

✍ Writing

1. Have students do the Writing as you go around the room to monitor progress.

2. Correct Writing as a class.

Extension Activity: Write a Story

1. Tell the class that they are writing a story about their class. Ask them what they want to include.

2. Elicit such things as:
> This is our English class.
> Our teacher is _____ .
> The class is in Room _____ .
> It is from _____ o'clock to _____ o'clock.
> It is a good class.

3. Write the sentences the students generate on the board.

4. Have class read the story aloud together, then individually.

5. Have class copy the story; then read the story to a partner.

Page 70   **A. Write the correct letter next to the occupation.**

Have students look at the picture and choose the correct occupation.

Page 71   **B. Write the missing words.**

Have students look at the pictures and fill in the blanks. Do #1 as an example.

Page 72   **C. Look at the pictures. Change the sentences.**

1. Go over #1. Explain that there are two people pictured and the sentence should be changed to plural.

2. Have students write the sentences.

3. Have pairs check their work, or correct by writing the sentences on the board or a transparency. Point out the contraction and the plural –s.

Page 73   **D. Look at the pictures. Answer the questions.**

Have students answer with yes or no and then a complete sentence. Do the exercise orally first if necessary.

What's His Name?

Communication Objective:
   Ask for and give others' names

New Structures:
   Possessives *his, her*

Visuals:
   V38   Her name's Sue Duran.
   V39   His name's Ben Lee.
   V40   Let's Talk: What's Her Name?

Page 74

✔ Review: Occupations

1. Draw the interaction grid on the board. Explain what students will be doing in each section: asking the names of persons they are interviewing, asking yes/no questions about the listed occupations, listening for the answer and checking the Yes or No column, and writing down the real occupation of four students in the class.

2. Have students practice asking questions, then have them walk around the room to do the activity, filling in information on the grid in the book.

3. After completing the activity, have volunteers tell the class what they learned about some students' occupations.

Page 75

Something New: His and Her

1. Show V38–39 and model the sentences. Emphasize the use of *his* and *her*.

2. Gesture to real students to practice the structure.

3. Add *my* and *your* to the practice with *his* and *her*.

☞ Practice Activity: My name's Sue

1. Give each student the opportunity to practice by forming groups of three or four.

2. Have each student practice using possessive adjective forms, using gestures to show who they're talking about.

 Let's Talk: What's Her Name*

1. Show V40 to establish the context of the conversation.

2. Model the dialogue as students listen, indicating the speakers by pointing to the visual or other means.

3. Model the dialogue again.

4. Model the dialogue and have class repeat.

5. Take one role and have class take other role; then change roles.

6. Divide class in half and have them take the two roles; then have then switch roles.

7. Have volunteers say the dialogue for the class.

 8. Have class open books and practice the dialogue in pairs.

*Cassette users can have students listen to the dialogue first with books closed.

Page 76 ☛ **Practice: "What's his name?"**

 1. Draw a rough sketch on the board showing the two women students discussing a good–looking male student.

2. Practice the dialogue in usual manner.

3. Do the same for the second Practice dialogue.

 4. Have class open books and read the first two pages of the lesson in pairs.

Extension Activity

1. Ask some students their addresses and phone numbers.

2. Write the responses on the board, then ask the class, "What's his/her/name/address/phone number?"

 3. Have class practice asking "What's your/his/her…?" as a class; then form small groups to practice asking and answering those questions.

★ Something Extra: Pronunciation

1. Introduce the pronunciation practice by explaining the slashes / / as symbols signifying pronunciation, not letters. Explain the /I/ sound, pronouncing it and saying that it is a short sound. Gesture to indicate "short."

2. Model the word "his," having students listening but not repeating. Using the illustrations in the book or V20 and V24 (from Lesson 7), model the sentences "His name's Ben Lee/Joe Martin."

3. Introduce the second sound /iy/ by pronouncing it, explaining and gesturing that it is a long sound.

4. Model the word "he's," having students listen. Use the visuals to model the sentences, "He's a waiter/salesclerk."

5. On the board make two columns, #1 for /I/ and #2 for /iy/. Write the appropriate word under it.

6. Ask students to indicate the sound they hear by putting up one or two fingers, and pronounce the words several times, monitoring class comprehension of the activity and discrimination of the two sounds.

[Note: If students are having trouble discriminating between the sounds, repeat the listening steps above on subsequent days to build their skill.]

7. Then direct the class to respond to the sounds they hear by finishing a phrase, saying "name" when they hear "his" or "waiter" when they hear "He's."

8. Now model and have class repeat the sound, word, and sentence in the first column; then the second column.

9. Then have class repeat each sound, word, and sentence across the columns: /I/, then /iy/; His, then He's, etc.

Page 77 ☛ **Practice Activity: I think it's his pen**

1. Have class form small groups. Gather common objects belonging to students in the groups and place them in front of the group.

2. Explain that students will practice asking about the objects, in order to find the owner of object.

3. Have class practice example dialogue, practicing with some objects and students before asking all students to practice.

★ Something Extra: Writing

Direct students who finish the writing activity ahead of other students to go ahead with this extra activity. This need not be corrected as a whole class activity, but you may wish to check on the work done by those who were able to get to it.

Page 78 📼 **Reading:** Two Students*

1. Ask students to read the story independently, then ask yes/no and other comprehension questions about the story.

2. Ask a volunteer or two to tell the story to the class.

3. Then have the whole class and/or pairs read the story.

*Cassette users can have students listen to the Reading first with books closed.

✑ Writing

1. Have class do Writing activity independently, helping students who need it.

2. Correct Writing as a class.

Lesson 9 Activity Pages

Page 79 ***A. Look at the picture and write the correct word.***
1. Lead a discussion about each picture.

2. Have students fill in the blanks.

3. Read the story aloud to check.

4. Optional: Have students read the story aloud to each other in pairs.

Page 80 ***B. Write the words in the boxes. Listen and circle the words you hear. Three circles in a row=BINGO!!***
1. Instruct students to copy the words from the word list onto the BINGO grid in random order. Each person's resulting grid should be different. You can model this by doing it more than once on the board or a transparency, putting the words in different order each time.
[Note: it's easiest if students go down the word list in order and place the words in the boxes randomly.]

Unit Three Evaluation

Page 81 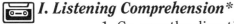 ***I. Listening Comprehension****

1. Go over the directions for Part I with students.

2. Read each item of the script two times, at normal conversational speed.

Script:

1. She's a homemaker.

2. He's a salesclerk.

3. They're waiters.

4. She's a dentist.

5. They're barbers.

6. Is he a teacher?

7. Is she a cook?

8. Are you students?

9. Are they doctors?

10. Are they bakers?

*Cassette users can have students listen to the script on the tape.

Page 82 & 83 ***II. Reading and III. Writing***

1. Go over the directions for Parts II and III with students.

2. Have class do these sections independently.

Evaluation Check

1. Correct evaluation by having student volunteers write their answers on the board or an overhead transparency.

2. Have class check their answers.

3. Circulate to make sure students have checked their work accurately.

Lesson 10

How Much Is It?

Communication Objectives:
Identify coins and their values
Identify break–time food items
Ask for and give prices
Order food items by size

New Structures:
Determiner *this*
Questions with *how much*
Partitives *a cup of/a bottle of/a can of*
Adjectives *small, medium, large*

Visuals:
V41	a penny
V42	a nickel
V43	a dime
V44	a quarter
V45	a half–dollar
V46	a doughnut
V47	a muffin
V48	small, medium, large cups of coffee
V49	bottles of apple juice and orange juice
V50	cans of Cal–Cola and Lemon–Up
V51	Let's Talk: How Much Is It?

Other instructional aids:
Realia (if available)—Coins
Foam cups in three sizes
Cans of soft drinks

Page 86

✔ Review: Names and Occupations

1. Get selected occupation visuals of men and women.

2. Write the names of each man and woman on four sheets of paper.

3. Have pairs of volunteers (one to "be" the person, the other the informant) come up and introduce the person to the class: e.g., "This is my friend. His name's _____ . He's a _____ ." The informant can also ask the class questions about the person. "What's his name? Is he a _____ ?" etc.

Something New: U.S. Coins

1. Put some coins in a pocket or in your hands and jiggle them so that the class can hear the coins.

2. Let the class identify what you have, then explain in simple terms that the lesson will be about coins and what they can buy with them.

3. Show visuals V41–45 one at a time, modeling vocabulary.

4. Test for comprehension of vocabulary by asking students to point to appropriate items as you say them, then ask yes/no and either/or questions about coins: e.g., "Is this a dime?" "Is this a nickel or quarter?"

5. Model vocabulary and have class repeat.

6. Ask what each item is: "What's this?" for class, groups, individuals to answer.

7. Repeat procedure, giving the value of each coin: e.g., "This is a penny. A penny is one cent. etc." Ask: "How much is a dime?" for class to answer: "10 cents" etc.

Page 87   ## ☞ Practice: "What's this?"

1. Drill "What...?" and "How much...?"

2. Have class open books and read what they have been practicing, as a class and/or in pairs.

Something New: Food Items

1. Show visuals V46–50 one at a time, on modeling vocabulary.

2. Model vocabulary and have class repeat.

3. Drill "What...?" and "How much...?" again with the food and drink items.

4. Model and practice the questions "What is this?" and "How much is it?" with the same items.

5. Direct pairs or groups to do the same questions and answers with the items pictured in their books.

Let's Talk: How Much Is It?*

1. Look at your wristwatch or at clock on the wall and pretend that it's time for the break.

2. Show V51A to show that the dialogue takes place at a catering truck or wherever the students buy snacks during breaks.

3. Model the dialogue as students listen, indicating the speakers by pointing to the visual or other means.

4. Model the dialogue again.

5. Model the dialogue and have class repeat.

6. Take one role and have class take other role; then change roles.

7. Divide class in half and have them take the two roles; then have them switch roles.

8. Have volunteers say the dialogue for the class.

 9. Have class open books and practice the dialogue in pairs.

*Cassette users can have students listen to the dialogue first with books closed.

☛ **Practice: "It's a bottle of orange juice"**

 1. Using visuals as cues, have class practice, using substitutions and question and answer drills.

2. Be sure to practice asking and answering the following:
    What's this?
    What size is this (cup)?
    How much is it?

 3. Open books and have class read what they have been practicing.

■ **Interaction:** At the Food Truck

1. Explain to class that they will practice buying food from a truck or lunch counter at school.

2. Elicit from class what kind of questions they will ask for information about the food items, how these questions can be answered.
[Note: Depending on comfort level of students and their practicing questions and answers without "scripts," you can choose to write sample questions and answers on the board, or not.]

3. Practice asking and answering questions.

4. Divide classroom into areas where students can roleplay being customers and order takers.

5. Have volunteers be order takers, and have rest of students go up to each "truck" or "counter" and give their orders.

Page 90 📼 **Reading:** The Lunch Truck*

1. Have class look at the illustration and establish context for story.

2. Have students read the story by themselves.

3. Go over the discussion questions, starting with comprehension questions about the story; then encourage students to share their experiences about lunch trucks.

4. Have class read story together as a class, in groups, and/or individually.

*Cassette users can have students listen to the story while reading silently.

✎ **Writing**

1. Have students do writing activity independently, helping students who need it.

2. Correct Writing as a class.

3. Optional: Do a dictation of a dialogue at a lunch truck or a lunch counter that includes questions and answers like those in the Interaction above.

Page 91 ■ **Interaction:** How Many Coins Do You Have?

1. Ask students how many coins they have.

2. Let them work in pairs or small groups and count the number of pennies, nickels, etc., they have, and what the value of the coins is.

3. Have groups report back to class and determine who is the "richest" person in class.

Page 92 A. Listen. Write the correct letter.*

1. Go over the directions. Read #1 as an example and make sure students understand the task.

2. Play the tape or read the script at normal conversational speed.

Script:
1. A: How much is a bottle of orange juice?
   B: It's 80 cents
   A: How much?
   B: 80 cents.

2. A: How much is a bottle of apple juice?
   B: It's 75 cents.
   A: How much?
   B: 75 cents.

3. A: How much is a small cup of coffee?
   B: It's 35 cents.
   A: How much?
   B: 35 cents.

4. A: How much is a large cup of tea?
   B: It's 60 cents.
   A: How much?
   B: 60 cents

5. A: How much is a can of Cal–Cola?
   B: It's 65 cents.
   A: How much?
   B: 65 cents.

*Cassette users can have students listen to the script on tape.

Page 93 **B. Write the question.**

1. Go over the three questions and explain that students should choose the appropriate question for each answer and write it in the blank.

2. Have students work independently.

3. Correct by writing the questions on the board or a transparency, or by having students ask and answer questions in pairs. Note that the last two questions in item 8 can be *What size is it?* and *How much is it?*

Lesson 11

How Much Is That Binder?

Communication Objectives:
Identify bills and their values
Identify school supplies
Ask for and give prices
Use *Oh, good!* and *Oh, my!* to react to prices

New Structures:
Determiners *this/that*
Adjectives *cheap, expensive*

Visuals:
V52   a one–dollar bill
V53   a five–dollar bill
V54   a ten–dollar bill
V55   a twenty–dollar bill
V56   Let's Talk: How Much Is That Binder?

Other instructional aids:
Realia—Textbook
Notebook
Pen, pencil
Dictionary
Binder and binder paper
Real bills

✔ Review

1. Use V41–45 from the previous lesson to practice names of coins and their values.

2. Have class practice total amounts of different numbers of coins: e.g., "How much are 3 dimes, 2 nickels, and 4 pennies?"

Page 94 ## Something New: U.S. Money—Bills and Coins

 1. Show real paper money; elicit from class what the bills are.

2. Explain to class that they will learn about bills.

3. Show visuals V52–55, of U.S. bills, to introduce vocabulary and check comprehension.

4. Have students practice the vocabulary by listening and repeating.

5. Introduce the idea that one dollar is equal to one hundred cents.

6. Roughly draw 4 quarters, then 2 quarters, 5 dimes, then 3 quarters, two dimes, and a nickel on the board.
> Ask: "How many coins are there?" and "How much is it?" for each picture to show that 100 cents are equal to one dollar.

7. Show the dollar bill and the various coins equaling a dollar and explain that they are the same amount.

8. Have students open their books and read what they have been practicing orally.

Page 95 ## Something New: It's $1.75

1. If there is a bookstore on site, use it to explain the setting.

2. Use realia or borrow student book, notebook, binder, etc. to practice the vocabulary.

3. Draw the items on the board and add the price of each one above or below the item. Note: Draw the items in two groups with some items near where you're standing and some items farther away in order to teach:
> *this:* notebook, book, pen
> *that:* binder, paper, dictionary, pencil

4. Stand next to items denoting *this* in the lesson. Say: "This notebook is 1 dollar and 75 cents." Go over the cost of all three of the items near you. Staying where you are, point to each of the items that are farther away, saying the cost with *that*.

5. Have the students repeat, using gestures for *this* and *that*.

6. Check for comprehension by asking questions.

7. Go over the cost of each item again. This time teach students how to say it "the short way." Say: "This notebook is 1 dollar and 75 cents. It's one seventy–five." Go over the cost of each item, first using the words dollars and cents, then the short way. Give students the opportunity to say the cost of items both ways.

8. Have students open books to read what they have been practicing orally.

Extension Activity

If more practice is needed on *this* and *that,* gather a few of the items in the front of the room and a few items in another part of the room. Say "This is a _____ " for items near you and "That is a _____ " for items far from you.

Then have individual students do the same thing. You can have them move next to one area or the other, or you can hand them items for *this* and have them talk about items that are farther away for *that.*

Page 96

☛ Practice: "It's a binder"

Have pairs do the Practice. After they finish #1 to #4, they can continue making up questions and answers about the items on the board.

▣ Let's Talk: How Much Is That Binder?*

1. Show V56 to establish the context of the conversation. Explain the situation.

2. Model the dialogue as students listen, indicating the speakers by pointing to the visual or other means.

3. Model the dialogue again.

4. Model the dialogue and have class repeat.

5. Take one role and have class take other role; then change roles.

6. Divide class in half and have them take the two roles; then have them switch roles.

7. Have volunteers say the dialogue for the class.

*Cassette users can have students listen to the dialogue first with books closed.

Page 97

☛ Practice: "It's three ninety–five"

Have class open books and practice the dialogue and the following Practice: "It's three ninety–five" in pairs.

Extension Activity

1. Have students help you make small pieces of paper to write the cost of items.

2. Form groups and have each group gather items: pen, pencil, notebook, etc., for the activity.

3. Have students write the cost of items on paper and put one on each item.

4. Have students practice asking and answering questions and roleplay being clerks and customers in bookstore. Encourage them to make judgments about whether they think items are cheap or expensive.

☛ **Practice Activity: Prices**

1. Dictate to students the price of each item listed.

2. Use the first item for practice.

3. Use the following amounts for each item, or make up your own:
   1. book $6.50
   2. pencil   10 cents
   3. notebook $2.25
   4. dictionary $8.60
   5. binder $4.40
   6. pen $1.49

4. Correct activity as a class.

📼 **Reading:** The Student Bookstore*

1. Introduce Reading activity by looking at illustration.

2. Have class read independently. Then read to the students as they listen.

3. Ask comprehension questions and then discuss other things pertaining to bookstores: items for sale, what they think is cheap or expensive, etc.

4. Read the story aloud as a class, either from the book or from a transparency.

*Cassette users can have students listen to the tape after looking at the illustration.

✐ **Writing:** Westside Adult School Bookstore

1. Introduce Writing activity by having class look at the name of the school. (It's a different school from the one in the reading.)

2. Encourage the students to read the story on their own and fill in the missing words independently.

3. Circulate and give help to those who need it.

4. When class has completed the activity, correct the story together. Use the story as another reading activity, reading it as a class, in groups, or in pairs.

56   Delta's Apple Pie, Teacher's Guide 1A

Page 99   **A. Read the sentence and circle the correct letter.**

1. Go over the directions and do #1 as an example. If you feel the exercise will be challenging, do #2 as an example as well.

2. Have students work independently.

3. Correct as a class.

Page 100   **B. Work with a partner. Ask "How much is a _____ ?"**

1. Explain that one partner will ask the question and the other will make up the price of the item. Model a few times.

2. Have students work in pairs, first one and then the other asking the questions.

C. Listen and write the prices on the receipts.*

1. Use the pictures to explain the meaning of receipt. Explain that students will write the prices they hear on the receipts in the book.

2. Play the tape or read the script at normal conversational speed. Read each item as many times as necessary, each time at normal speed.

Script:

1. Okay, let's see…that's one binder at 2 dollars and 50 cents, paper at 2 dollars and 25 cents, one pen at 75 cents, one pencil at 15 cents and one dictionary at 3 dollars and 95 cents. So let me add that together…your total is 9 dollars and 60 cents.

2. All right, let's see what you have…one textbook at 8 dollars, one notebook at 2.75, 2 pencils at 30 cents, and one dictionary at 2.90. That makes a total of 14 dollars and 25 cents.

3. Let's take a look at these things…hmmm. 2 pens, that's 75 and 75; 2 binders, at 3 dollars each; one textbook, that's 7.95; and one dictionary at 3.95. That comes to a total of 19 dollars and 40 cents.

*Cassette users can have students listen to the script on tape.

D. Circle the correct change.

1. Explain that students will read the price the cashier is saying in each picture, look at how much money the customer has in hand, and then choose the answer with the correct amount of change the cashier needs to give back. Do #1 as an example.

2. Have students work alone or in pairs.

3. Go over each item with the class to correct.

4. Optional: Have volunteers roleplay the cashier/customer interaction and practice making change. They can use real money or they can say the amounts and the class can check the amount of change given.

Lesson 12

For Here or To Go?

Communication Objectives:
> Order fast–food items
> Take orders for fast–food items
> Distinguish between numbers *15/50, 16/60*, etc.

New Structures:
> *May I*…for taking an order

Visuals:
> V57   a hamburger
> V58   a cheeseburger
> V59   a hot dog
> V60   french fries
> V61   a carton of milk
> V62   Let's Talk: For Here or To Go?

Other instructional aids:
> Realia—Classified ads
> > Tray (or flat surface to simulate tray)
> > Paper bag

Page 102   ✔ **Review:** Money

1. Establish context by asking how people find jobs. Explain that it is possible to find jobs through the newspaper.

2. Show classified ads, if available. Read sample pay.

3. Have class open their books and elicit from class the pay of each of the workers listed in classified ads.

4. Give students opportunity to say pay amounts with dollars and cents as well as the short way.

Page 103   **Something New:** Fast Food

 1. Explain lesson objective in simple terms.

2. Use V57–61 to present vocabulary.

☞ Practice Activity: Ordering fast food

1. Put the wall menu on a transparency or on board and show, or have students open their books to the wall menu.

2. Go over the menu together.

3. Ask comprehension questions about the menu, asking about sizes, cost, kinds of items there are.

4. Have students practice asking and answering discussion questions in pairs.

Page 104 **Let's Talk:** For Here or To Go?*

1. Show V62 to establish the context of the conversation. Teach meaning of "For here or to go?" using a tray (simulation) for "for here" and a paper bag for "to go."

2. Model the dialogue as students listen, indicating the speakers by pointing to the visual or other means.

3. Model the dialogue again.

4. Model the dialogue and have class repeat.

5. Take one role and have class take other role; then change roles.

6. Divide class in half and have them take the two roles; then have them switch roles.

7. Have volunteers say the dialogue for the class.

 8. Have class open books and practice the dialogue and the following Practice in pairs.

*Cassette users can have students listen to the dialogue first with books closed.

■ Interaction: At a Fast-Food Restaurant

1. Go over ways to practice being a customer and an order taker.

2. Have class practice in pairs.

3. Have a few volunteers come up in front of class and do the roleplay.

Delta's Apple Pie, Teacher's Guide 1A

📼 **Reading:** The Fast Life*

1. Introduce the topic by asking class if there are fast–food eating places in their own country and elicit what they are.

2. Have class read story independently.

3. Ask comprehension questions about the story. Explain simply the vocabulary words—life, cars, airplanes. Use a rough drawing of the world to show where the countries Japan, England, and France are.

4. Go over the questions for discussion.

5. Read story as a class.

*Cassette users can have students listen to the Reading on tape after step 1.

Page 105
■ **Interaction:** May I Take Your Order?

1. Explain the grid and the example.

 2. Have class walk around the room and speak to three people to complete the activity.

✎ **Writing**

Have class do Writing independently; then correct as a class.

Page 106
★ **Something Extra:** Pronunciation

1. Write the numbers for Counting by Tens on the board.

2. Model the numbers, pointing to each.

3. Have class repeat the numbers.

4. Write the "–teen" numbers on the board in a second column, model the numbers, and have class repeat. [Note: match the –teen numbers with the numbers from thirty through ninety.]

5. Point to numbers randomly and have class, groups, individuals say them.

6. Ask class to tell which number they hear, one from the first or second column, by indicating the column with their fingers.

7. Model some numbers, monitoring how well students can discriminate between the tens and the teens. Concentrate on 50/15 sounds, which are difficult for students.

8. Give a dictation on ten of the numbers; correct as a class. (Dictate numbers that you find the class having difficulty hearing.)

Lesson 12 Activity Page

Page 107

A. Talk about the picture.

1. Have students talk about what the people are doing and about the food items and prices on the sign. Model a few questions about the picture.

2. Have students work in pairs.

B. Look at the picture. Read the questions. Circle the answers.

1. Read the directions together. Do #1 as an example.

2. Have students work independently.

3. Correct as a class.

C. Look at the picture. Write two questions and answer the questions.

1. Go over the example. Explain that students will write questions and answers.

2. Have students work independently. Circulate around the room to check their work and offer help.

3. Correct by having pairs check each other's work and then practice reading both partners' work in pairs.

Unit Four Evaluation

Page 109 **I. Listening Comprehension***

      1. Go over the directions for Part I with students.

      2. Read each item of the script two times, at normal conversational speed.

Script:

      1. It's a dime.

      2. It's fifty cents.

      3. How much is it?

      4. How much is a bottle of apple juice?

      5. It's a five dollar bill.

      6. How much is this?

      7. What's that?

      8. How much is that?

      *Cassette users can have students listen to the script on tape.

Page 110 **II. Reading and III. Writing**

      1. Go over the directions for Parts II and III with students.

      2. Have class do these sections independently.

Evaluation Check

      1. Correct evaluation by having student volunteers write their answers on the board or an overhead transparency.

      2. Have class check their answers.

      3. Circulate to make sure students have checked their work accurately.

Lesson 13

Tuesday's My Day Off

Communication Objectives:
> Identify days of the week
> Talk about days off from work
> Use ordinal numbers to talk about dates

New Structures:
> Questions with *when*
> Preposition of time *on*

Visuals:
> V63   Calendar for January
> V64   Let's Talk: Tuesday Is My Day Off

Page 112 ✔ **Review:** Fast Foods

1. Show wall menu for MacBurger's from previous lesson on chalkboard or overhead.

2. Have students take role of clerk and customers, placing orders "for here" or "to go."

Something New: A Calendar

 1. Present the objectives to the class as stated in the lesson.

2. Establish context:

> T: What's today? It's *Monday*.
> What day of the week is it? It's Monday.
> There are seven days in a week: Sunday, Monday, etc.
> This is the calendar for the month of January.
> See the days of the week on this page?

3. Have students repeat the days of the week.

4. Show the calendar visual, V63, on overhead or write the days of the week on the chalkboard. Write down the usual abbreviations for the days of the week.

☛ **Practice: "What day is it?"**

1. Mark a calendar on the transparency or chalkboard and lead the practice.

2. Provide students with opportunity to ask as well as answer questions.

 3. Have students open their books and read what they've been practicing orally.

 Let's Talk: Tuesday Is My Day Off*

1. Show V64 and establish context.

2. Lead discussion on days off from work.

3. Model the dialogue as students listen, indicating the speakers by pointing to the visual or other means.

4. Model the dialogue again.

5. Model the dialogue and have class repeat.

6. Take one role and have class take other role; then change roles.

7. Divide class in half and have them take the two roles; then have them switch roles.

8. Have volunteers say the dialogue for the class.

 9. Have class open books and practice the dialogue in pairs.

*Cassette users can have students listen to the dialogue first with books closed.

☛ **Practice: "When is your day off?"**

1. Have several rows (or groups) practice the exchanges, using real information.

2. Start the chain by asking the first student in each group, "When is your day off?"

☛ **Practice: "See you on Tuesday, then"**

1. Have students practice as a chain drill or in pairs.

2. Have students open their books and read what they've been practicing orally.

★ **Something Extra:** Ordinal Numbers

1. Establish context: Show the calendar for January. Explain how ordinal numbers are used in conversations about the days of a month.

2. Present the ordinal numbers from 1st to 31st.

Page 115 ## ☛ **Practice: "What's the date today?"**

1. Point to dates on the calendar and ask:

> T: What's the date today?

2. Have volunteers come to the front of the room and point to dates and ask the questions.

☛ **Practice: "What day is the 20th?"**

1. Point to the days on the calendar and ask:

> T: What day is the 20th?

2. Have volunteers point to dates and ask the questions.

3. Have students open their books and read what they have been practicing.

Extension Activity: Writing Dates

Demonstrate to class the way dates are written in English:

> January 31, 1994 or 1–31–94 or 1/31/94

Page 116 ## ■ **Interaction:** Standing in Line

1. Have 7 volunteers line up in front of the room.

2. Follow the directions in the lesson.

🎦 **Reading:** Time for School*

1. Have class look at illustration; then read the passage independently.

2. Ask comprehension questions.

3. Discuss school days for students' own class.

4. Have class read the story together.

5. Have students volunteer to read segments aloud.

66   Delta's Apple Pie, Teacher's Guide 1A

6. Have students ask each other discussion questions in pairs.

*Cassette users can have students listen to the Reading after looking at the illustration.

Page 117 ✍ **Writing**

1. Have students complete the exercise.

2. Go over the answers together.

Lesson 13 Activity Pages

Page 118 ▭ ***A. Listen and circle the correct days.****

1. Go over the directions and the example.

2. Play the tape or read the script at normal speed.

Script:

1. My day off is Friday.

2. Sam's day off is Thursday.

3. Rosa's day off is Tuesday.

4. Ben's day off is Saturday.

5. Don's day off is Wednesday.

6. May's days off are Saturday and Sunday.

7. Tony's days off are Sunday and Monday.

8. Ruben's days off are Thursday and Friday.

*Cassette users can have students listen to the script on tape.

Page 119 ***B. Talk about the picture.***

Have students discuss the picture in pairs, or lead a discussion with the whole class. Include *first*, *second*, *third*, etc. to talk about the people in line.

C. Choose the correct word. Fill in the blanks.

1. Go over the directions

2. Have pairs or individuals fill in the blanks.

3. Correct by reading the story aloud.

When Is Your Birthday?

Communication Objectives:
    Identify months of the year
    Talk about birthdays

New Structures:
    Questions with *how old*

Visuals:
    V65   calendar for one year
    V66   Let's Talk: When Is Your Birthday?

Other instructional aids:
    Realia—A calendar

Page 120

✔ Review: Days of the Week and Ordinal Numbers

Follow the steps as outlined in the lesson.

Something New: The Months of the Year

1. Present the objectives to the class as stated in the lesson.

2. Establish the context by showing a calendar. Flip the calendar (or point to V65) and name the months of the year.

3. Have students repeat.

4. Write the months on the chalkboard and practice.

5. If you wish, write the abbreviations for the months and have students copy.

Page 121

☛ Practice: "What's the 3rd month of the year?"

1. Flip the calendar and start the practice.

2. Have volunteers take turns flipping the calendar and asking:
        S1: What's the 3rd month of the year? etc.

☛ **Practice: "What's the date?"**

    1. Use the calendar and start the practice by pointing to dates at random.

    2. Have students take turns doing the same.

 3. Have students open the books and read the exercises.

 Let's Talk: When Is Your Birthday?*

    1. Show V66 and establish context.

    2. Lead discussion on birthdays.

    3. Model the dialogue as students listen, indicating the speakers by pointing to the visual or other means.

    4. Model the dialogue again.

    5. Model the dialogue and have class repeat.

    6. Take one role and have class take other role; then change roles.

    7. Divide class in half and have them take the two roles; then have them switch roles.

    8. Have volunteers say the dialogue for the class.

 9. Have class open books and practice the dialogue in pairs.

    *Cassette users can have students listen to the dialogue first with books closed.

Page 122 ☛ **Practice: "It's on May 1st"**

    1. Point to a date on the calendar and ask: "When is Mario's birthday?"

    2. Give students opportunity to ask and answer questions.

    3. Have students open their books and read the exercises.

■ **Interaction:** What's Your Birthday Month?

    1. Have 12 students make a sign for each month on a sheet of paper.

    2. Place the signs around the room.

    3. Have the students stand by their birthday months.

4. Have students ask each other their birthdays.

5. Have them stand in order of their birthdays.

Page 123 🔊 **Reading:** Happy Birthday, Mr. Wong*

1. Have students look at the Reading illustration and discuss birthdays.

2. Have students read independently.

3. Ask comprehension questions.

4. Have class read the dialogue together.

5. Have volunteers take roles.

6. Have students ask each other the discussion questions.

*Cassette users can have students listen to the Reading first with books closed.

✐ **Writing**

1. Have students write independently.

2. Go over the answers together.

Extension Activity

If time permits, lead a discussion on some important birthdates for people in the U.S. as well as in students' native countries.

Page 124 ★ **Something Extra:** Birthdays of Presidents

1. Give a brief explanation of Presidents Washington and Lincoln and their role in U.S. history.

2. Show the calendar for February with Washington's and Lincoln's birthdays highlighted.

☞ **Practice: "Yes, they are"**

1. Give students the opportunity to ask and answer questions.

2. Have students open their books and read the exercises.

Lesson 14 Activity Pages

Page 125 **A. Look at the calendar. Listen and circle the dates you hear.***

    1. Explain that students will circle the date they hear on the calendar in the book.

    2. Play the tape or read the script at normal speed.

> **Script:**
>
> This is the month of February. There are a lot of holidays in February. Circle the 12th, that's Lincoln's birthday. On the 12th we celebrate the birthday of Abraham Lincoln, the 16th President of the United States.
>
> Circle the 22nd of February. The 22nd is George Washington's birthday. We celebrate his birthday in the United States because he was our first president.
>
> Circle the 14th of February. This is a special day. It's Valentine's Day. On the 14th we give cards, flowers or candy to people we love.
>
> Circle the 29th of February. The 29th of February is called Leap Day. February has 28 days most of the time, but every 4th year, there is an extra day…the 29th.
>
> Circle the 17th. This is a very special day. In fact, the 17th of February is my favorite day. It's my birthday! Happy birthday to me!

    *Cassette users can have students listen to the script on tape.

    3. Have students compare their calendars to check, or circle the answers on a transparency of page 125.

B. Look at the calendar and write the days and ordinal numbers.

Have students fill in the blanks according to the calendar.

C. Write the months next to the dates.

    1. Review the months and their spelling.

    2. Have students work independently.

    3. Correct as a class. Note that July 4, 1776 is the "birthday" of the United States.

D. Listen and do it.*

        1. Explain that students will listen and then circle or draw something on the picture.

        2. Play the tape or read the script at normal speed. Repeat as many times as necessary.

> **Script:**
> 1. Look at the balloons. There are 3 balloons. Circle the 3rd balloon.
>
> 2. Look at the presents. There are 4 presents. Circle the 2nd present.
>
> 3. Look at the party hats. Do you see 5? Circle the 4th hat.
>
> 4. There are 8 candles on this cake. Put two more candles on the cake. There are 10 candles now.
>
> 5. Do you see the bottles of juice? Apple and orange? Circle the first bottle.
>
> 6. Look at the hamburgers on the 1st plate. Are you hungry? Put two hamburgers on the second plate.

    *Cassette users can have students listen to the script on tape.

E. Look at the picture and follow the directions.

        1. Discuss the picture with the whole class.

        2. Have individuals read instructions 1–7 and write or draw on the picture as directed, or have pairs give instructions to each other, or read the instructions aloud and have the whole class follow the instructions.

Lesson 15

Where Are You From?

Communication Objectives:
> Name cities, states, and countries
> Ask for and give native country

New Structures:
> Questions with *where*
> Preposition of place *from*

Visuals:
> V67   map of the world
> V68   Let's Talk: Where Are You From?
> V69   Map of the U.S.

Other instructional aids:
> Wall map of the world
> Wall map of the United States

Page 128

✔ Review: When Is Your Birthday?

> 1. Have volunteers write their birthdays on the chalkboard.

> 2. Have class read the dates aloud.

Something New: The Map of the World

> 1. Present the objectives as stated in the lesson.

> 2. Use a wall map or a globe, if available. Otherwise, show V67 on a transparency or tack it to a wall.

> 3. Point out the United States of America and the city of Los Angeles. (Follow the student book. Use the terms country, state, and city.)

> 4. Point out the location of the class.

Page 129

☞ Practice Activity: My native country

> 1. Ask students to call out the names of their native countries.

> 2. Ask volunteers to go to the map and point out their native countries and cities.

Let's Talk: Where Are You From?*

1. Show V68 to establish the context of the conversation: Three students are talking in the hall during the break.

2. Model the dialogue as students listen, indicating the speakers by pointing to the visual or other means.

3. Model the dialogue again.

4. Model the dialogue and have class repeat.

5. Divide class in three groups and have them take the three roles; then have them switch roles.

6. Have volunteers say the dialogue for the class.

7. Have class open books and practice the dialogue in pairs.

*Cassette users can have students listen to the dialogue first with books closed.

Page 130 ## ☞ Practice: "Where are you from?"

1. Have several rows (or groups) practice the exchange, using real information.

2. Start the chain by asking the first student in each group, "Where are you from?"

☞ Practice: "What city are you from?"

1. Follow the procedure of the previous exercise.

2. Have students open their books and read the exercises.

★ Something Extra: The United States of America

1. Show V69 on the overhead or use a wall map.

2. Locate the state the class is located in.

3. Point out some of the states of the union, highlighting California, New York, Texas, and Illinois.

4. Point out the city the class is located in.

5. Point out Los Angeles, New York City, Dallas, and Chicago.

☞ **Practice: "What's your state?"**

    1. Cue with the map of the U.S. and initiate the exercise.

    2. Have students take turns giving cues and answers.

    3. Have students ask *Wh–* questions and *Yes/No* questions.

    4. Have students open their books and read the exercises.

■ Interaction: Where Are You From?

Have students follow the directions as stated in the lesson.

📼 Reading: We Are the World*

    1. Establish context for Reading selection.

    2. Have students read the passage independently.

    3. Ask comprehension questions.

    4. Have class read the passage orally.

    5. Have students discuss the story, using the discussion questions.

    *Cassette users can have students listen to the Reading first with books closed.

✐ Writing

    1. Have students write independently.

    2. Go over the answers together.

Page 133   **A. Read the questions. Write your answers. Then ask your partner the questions.**

1. Go over the directions.

2. Have individuals write answers to the questions.

3. Have pairs ask and answer the questions.

B. Ask four friends for the information on the grid. Write the answers on the grid.

1. Explain the interaction activity.

2. Practice the questions students will need to ask.

3. Have students move around the room, talk to four different people, and record their answers on the grid.

4. Bring whole class together and ask individual students about the people on their grids.

5. Optional: Have students practice writing sentences about the people on their grids.

Page 134   **C. BINGO: Read the directions and play.**

1. Explain that you will dictate 16 dates, and students will write them on the BINGO grid in random order. Demonstrate by saying a few dates (month and day) and writing them in various places on the grid in your book, on the board, or on a transparency.
[Note: students must write the dates in different places on their grids so they will end up with different BINGO cards. You can choose the dates to dictate.]

2. Begin the BINGO game. Read the dates again in random order, or draw slips of paper with the dates written on them. Have students circle each date as they hear it.

3. Have students shout "BINGO!" when they have four circles in a row, and give a prize or a big round of applause for the winner or winners.

Unit Five **Evaluation**

Page 135 **I. Listening Comprehension***

    1. Go over the directions for Part I with students.

    2. Read each item of the script two times, at normal conversational speed.

        Script:
        1. See you on Thursday.

        2. It's the 4th month of the year.

        3. It's October 30th.

        4. It's a state.

        5. It's a country.

        6. Her birthday's May 1st.

        7. His birthday's in February.

        8. Is Friday his day off?

    *Cassette users can have students listen to the script on the tape.

Page 136 **II. Reading and III. Writing**

    1. Go over the directions for Parts II and III with students.

    2. Have class do these sections independently.

Evaluation Check

    1. Correct evaluation by having student volunteers write their answers on the board or an overhead transparency.

    2. Have class check their answers.

    3. Circulate to make sure students have checked their work accurately.

It's a Fruit Salad

Communication Objectives:
>Identify fruits
>Ask for and give prices of produce
>Follow directions for preparing food

New Structures:
>Articles *a/an*

Visuals:

V70	an apple
V71	an orange
V72	a banana
V73	a pear
V74	a grapefruit
V75	a pineapple
V76	a watermelon
V77	a lemon
V78	Let's Talk: Is This a Fruit Salad?

Other instructional aids:
>Realia—Bowl
>>Knife
>>Spoon
>>Apple
>>Orange
>>Banana

>Large cards or 8 ½" x 14" paper folded in half
>Occupations visuals (select from V16–27)

Page 138 | ✔ **Review:** Introduce a Friend

1. Have students write their names, native countries and occupations on cards.

2. Have pairs exchange cards and practice introducing each other to the class.

Optional Review Activity

1. Prepare two sets of cards—one set for names of fictitious people (separate males and females), the other set for names of countries.

2. Get occupation visuals, V16–27, from Lesson 7.

3. Make three piles with above, putting them face down.

4. Have two students come to the front of the room, make a selection from each of the three piles and take turns "introducing" their friend to the class.

> S1: This is my friend, Ramon Martinez.
> He's from Peru. He's a waiter.
> SS: We're happy to meet you, Ramon.
> S2: And this is my friend, Marta Samar.
> She's from Poland. She's a doctor.

5. If you prepare sets of smaller cards, students can continue activity in small groups.

Something New: Names of Fruit

1. Briefly give the objectives of the lesson.

2. Use visuals V70–77 to present the vocabulary in the usual way:
Model as students listen; have students repeat, ask yes/no questions, ask either/or questions, ask wh– questions.

Page 139

☞ Practice: "It's an apple"

1. Hold one visual close to you. Place another at a distance.
Model "This is…" indicating the one close to you, and "That's a…" indicating the one farther away.

2. Repeat with other visuals.

3. Have students use gestures to indicate understanding of "this" and "that."

4. Have class, groups, individuals ask and answer the questions of the Practice activity.

5. Have students open their books and read what they have been practicing orally.

Let's Talk: Is This a Fruit Salad?*

1. Show V78 to establish the context of the dialogue: Sue is in the deli section of the market, looking at the salads. She is talking to the clerk.

2. Model the dialogue as students listen, indicating the speakers by pointing to the visual or other means.

3. Model the dialogue again.

4. Model the dialogue and have class repeat.

5. Take one role and have class take other role; then change roles.

6. Divide class in half and have them take the two roles; then have them switch roles.

7. Have volunteers say the dialogue for the class.

8. Have class open books and practice the dialogue in pairs.

*Cassette users can have students listen to the dialogue first with books closed.

Page 140

☛ Practice: "It's the same price"

Draw salads and prices on the board for the Practice exercise. Have student volunteers come up and practice asking and answering questions before reading the exercise with a partner.

Something New: Making a Fruit Salad

 (If possible, bring several apples, bananas, and oranges, along with a bowl, knife, and spoon to class.)

1. Tell the class that you're going to make a fruit salad and demonstrate the actions of making a fruit salad as illustrated:

Get a bowl, knife and spoon.

Get the fruit.

Peel the fruit.

Slice the banana.

Cut up the apple and orange.

Delta's Apple Pie, Teacher's Guide 1A

Put the fruit in the bowl.

Stir the fruit.

Serve the salad.

Eat the fruit salad. (Say: Oh, it's good/delicious/etc.)

2. Repeat the demonstration, having class act out the motions with you.

3. Go through the actions again, with the student repeating the words as they do the actions.

4. If you do not have realia, then have the students follow the pictures in the text, first to listen, then to listen and do, and then to repeat while performing the action.

Optional: Make a transparency of the pictures and cut them out, putting them randomly on an overhead projector. Have volunteers put the pictures in order and give directions.

 5. Write the steps of the activity and have the students copy the steps in their books or notebooks.

Page 141 ☞ **Practice: "Cut up the fruit"**

Show the students how to circle the correct answer by using the first one as a sample and have them do the rest independently.

☞ **Practice: "What's first?"**

Explain what to do and have individuals or pairs do the activity independently.

Page 142 ■ **Interaction:** How to Make a Fruit Salad

Have pairs of students tell each other how to make fruit salad.

☞ **Practice Activity: Giving directions**

1. Have students write down the directions they gave for the interaction activity above, using the words in the box.

2. Have partners check each other's work or correct as a class.

Page 143 📼 **Reading:** At the Cafeteria*

1. Ask students questions about the picture to prepare them for the Reading.
    Say: "Who do you see in the picture?"
        "Where is he?" etc.

2. Have students read independently.

3. Ask questions to test comprehension.

4. Read story together as a class, in groups and individually.

*Cassette users can have students listen to the story as they read along.

✎ **Writing**

Have class do activity independently before correcting as a class.

Delta's Apple Pie, Teacher's Guide 1A

Page 144 **A. Listen and draw what you hear.***

    1. Go over the directions.

    2. Play the tape or read the script at normal speed. Pause long enough for students to draw the item mentioned. Repeat each section as necessary, always at normal speed.

> **Script:**
> Look at this kitchen. It's 5:30 and Ann and Mary are making a fruit salad.
>
> Draw the time on the clock. (pause)
>
> Ann is sitting at the table. She is cutting an apple.
>
> Draw the apple. (pause)
>
> Can you see Mary? She's standing near the table. She is holding a bowl in her left hand.
>
> Draw the bowl. (pause)
>
> Mary is pointing to a banana on the table.
>
> Draw the banana. (pause)

    *Cassette users can have students listen to the script on tape.

B. Look at the picture. Write the missing words.

    1. Have students choose the correct word for each blank.

    2. Correct as a class.

    3. Have students listen and repeat the dialogue; then practice it in pairs.

Page 145 **C. Match the sentence to the picture.**

    1. Demonstrate in your book, or on a transparency of the page, by drawing a line from sentence 1 to the correct picture.

    2. Have students work independently, then compare with another student to check their answers.

Lesson 17

Rosa Buys Vegetables

Communication Objectives:
Identify vegetables
Buy vegetables at a produce stand
Pronounce plural –s

New Structures:
Determiners *these/those*
Adverbs *a pound/each*

Visuals:
V79   a carrot/carrots
V80   an onion/onions
V81   a pepper/peppers
V82   a cucumber/cucumbers
V83   a cabbage/cabbages
V84   Let's Talk: Rosa Buys Vegetables

Page 146

✔ Review: A Fruit Salad

1. Using realia and/or visuals from Lesson 16, create a fruit bowl, or have students look at the illustration in the book.

2. Have students form small groups and give each a large sheet of paper. Say:

> Draw a large bowl on your sheet of paper. Take turns drawing different kinds of fruit in the bowl, naming the fruit. Describe your fruit bowl to other groups.

Something New: Vegetables

 Using V79–83, introduce the vocabulary items.

Page 147

☛ Practice: "Are these onions?"

1. Hold one visual close to you and place one at a distance. Practice "These are…" and "Those are…"

2. Repeat with other visuals.

3. Have student volunteers hold a visual and identify their visual and then another visual held by another student, using "These …" and Those…" appropriately.

4. Have class practice asking questions as well as responses.

 5. Have class open their books and read the practice interchanges as a class and in pairs.

Let's Talk: Rosa Buys Vegetables*

1. Use V84 to establish the setting of the dialogue: A customer talking to a market clerk at a produce market.

2. Model the dialogue as students listen, indicating the speakers by pointing to the visual or other means.

3. Model the dialogue again.

4. Model the dialogue and have class repeat.

5. Take one role and have class take other role; then change roles.

6. Divide class in half and have them take the two roles; then have them switch roles.

7. Have volunteers say the dialogue for the class.

 8. Have class open books and practice the dialogue in pairs.

*Cassette users can have students listen to the dialogue first with books closed.

Page 148 ## ☛ Practice: "They're 60 cents each"

 1. Put the visuals up around the room, with prices attached to them. Have prices using the terms "each, pound, bunch."

 2. Have students practice asking and answering questions, using yes/no, either/or, and wh– questions. Then have class open their books and read what they have been practicing orally.

Reading: An Outdoor Market*

1. Introduce Reading activity by having class look at the illustration and discussing what the Reading will be about.

2. Have students read independently.

3. Ask comprehension questions.

4. Read the story together as a class.

5. Have students do the yes/no statement exercise independently before correcting it.

6. Go over the discussion questions as a class or in small groups.

*Cassette users can have students listen to the Reading after looking at the illustration.

Page 149   ✍ **Writing**

1. Have students complete the exercise.

2. Go over the exercise as a class.

Page 150   ★ **Something Extra:** Pronunciation

1. Explain that the "s" in a plural noun has three different sounds.

2. Write the symbols for the sounds on the chalkboard: /s/ /z/ and /ɪz/. (The diagonal slashes indicate sounds.)

3. Write the plural words from the lesson on the board, pronouncing them.

4. Write the plurals of classroom items from previous lessons, pronouncing them carefully.

5. Have class practice making the sounds, then the words.

6. Model the words, then phrases, and then sentences. Have class repeat.

7. Go over the first three words in the exercise, showing class how to write the sounds they hear.

8. Dictate the other words, having class write the plural sound they hear.

1. books /s/	6. apples /z/
2. pencils /z/	7. oranges /ɪz/
3. cabbages /ɪz/	8. desks /s/
4. bananas /z/	9. vegetables /z/
5. dentists /s/	10. lemons /z/

■ Interaction: A Market

1. Draw various vegetables on paper or on the chalkboard, or use the visuals to set up "a market" in the classroom.

2. Have students take turns being clerks and customers, asking and answering questions about the vegetables.

Lesson 17 Activity Pages

Page 151 **A. Listen and label the vegetables.***

1. Explain the situation: Mark has to label the boxes to show what kind of vegetables are inside. Students will listen and write down in the blanks what vegetables he sees in each group of boxes.

2. Play the tape or read the script. If repetition is necessary, play the whole section or read the whole script again.

> **Script:**
> Oh no! All the labels are gone. Now, what is in all these boxes?!! I'll have to open them and see. Hmm...
>
> There are carrots in the first group of boxes, next to me. I'll write carrots, C–A–R–R–O–T–S.
>
> There are onions in the group of boxes next to the carrots. I'll write onions. O–N–I–O–N–S.
>
> Cucumbers are in the third group of boxes. I'll write cucumbers. C–U–C–U–M–B–E–R–S.
>
> There are peppers in the boxes on the truck. I'll write peppers. P–E–P–P–E–R–S.
>
> *Cassette users can have students listen to the script on tape.

3. Correct as a class.

Page 152 **B. Look at the answer and write the question. Use "these" or "those."**
1. Go over the directions.

2. Have students work independently.

3. Have volunteers write the sentences on the board; then check them together.

4. Have students compare their answers to the corrected sentences on the board. Circulate to make sure they are correcting their work accurately.

Page 153   **C. Look at the vegetable bins. Read and follow the directions.**

Have students draw or write the items as instructed. Circulate to check their work.

Lesson 18

The Bakery

Communication Objectives:
Identify kinds of bakery items
Ask about items in a bakery
Make a polite request using *I'd like*
Confirm an order by repeating
Order a cake for a special occasion

New Structures:
Partitive *a loaf of*
Quantifier *a dozen*
Questions with *What kind of*
Adjective placement

Visuals:
V85   a cake
V86   a pie
V87   a loaf of bread
V88   hamburger buns
V89   hot dog buns
V90   a dozen doughnuts
V91   a dozen cookies
V92   Let's Talk: It's an Apple Pie

Other instructional aids:
Realia—A grocery bag

Page 154   ✔ **Review:** Fill the Grocery Bag

1. Show the grocery bag, or quickly draw a grocery bag on the board, and say, "Let's go to the market. What are we going to buy?"

2. Start out by suggesting "One cucumber." Then call on a student and prompt him/her to say "One cucumber and two…" Prompt another to continue with the sequence of numbers, adding another type of produce with the number.

3. This can be a whole class or a group activity.

Something New: Bakery Items

 Use V85–91 to present the new vocabulary.

Page 155 **Let's Talk:** It's an Apple Pie*

1. Show V92 to establish the context of the conversation.

2. Model the dialogue as students listen, indicating the speakers by pointing to the visual or other means.

3. Model the dialogue again.

4. Model the dialogue and have class repeat.

5. Take one role and have class take other role; then change roles.

6. Divide class in half and have them take the two roles; then have them switch roles.

7. Have volunteers say the dialogue for the class.

8. Have class open books and practice the dialogue in pairs.

*Cassette users can have students listen to the dialogue first with books closed.

Page 156 ☛ **Practice: "What kind of bread is this?"**

1. Use the illustrations to cue student practice: "What kind of…?" and yes/no questions with this/that, these/those.

2. Have class read what they have been practicing orally.

☛ **Practice: "May I help you today?"**

1. Have students practice using polite language: "May I help you?" and "I'd like…" to ask for a bakery item.

2. Focus on the use of repetition to indicate understanding of the request. Give students lots of opportunity to practice this communication strategy.

Page 157 ★ **Something Extra:** Cakes for Special Occasions

1. Elicit from students responses to the illustrated cakes.

2. Point out the various decorations on the cakes.

3. Discuss how these occasions might be celebrated, noting that a special dinner or party would require special food.

📼 Let's Talk: I'd Like a Cake for Saturday*

1. Show the illustration in the book to establish the context of the conversation.

2. Model the dialogue and have class repeat.

3. Have the students practice in pairs.

*Cassette users can have students listen to the dialogue first with books closed.

☛ Practice Activity

1. Model various substitutions for the missing items in the dialogue.

2. Have students work in pairs to roleplay the baker and customer, substituting different occasions and kinds of cakes.

3. Have volunteers present their roleplays to the class.

Page 158 ## 📼 Reading: An Anniversary Celebration*

1. Ask pre–reading questions using the illustration.

2. Have students read the story independently.

3. Ask comprehension questions; then ask the questions which ask students about their own experiences.

4. Have students working in pairs go over the questions, practicing asking and answering the questions.

*Cassette users can have the students listen to the Reading on tape after step 1.

✍ Writing

Follow the usual procedure for the Writing activity.

Extension Activity

1. Write the following recipe on the board and discuss the recipe: ingredients, how to make it, utensils to use, etc.

Recipe
No–Bake Cookies

1 cup	non–fat dry milk
1/2 cup	peanut butter
1/2 cup	honey

Optional toppings:
  coconut
  sesame seeds
  crushed granola cereal

Measure the ingredients. Put the ingredients into a bowl.
Mix all the ingredients together. Pick up a spoonful of the dough in your hands. Roll the dough into balls. Optional: Roll balls in one of the toppings.

2. Have volunteers bring the materials and ingredients necessary to make the cookies in class the next day.

3. Encourage class to plan a celebration and bring special sweets from their country to share with the class. Have them share the recipes too.

Lesson 18 Activity Pages

Page 159

A. Talk about the picture.

Initiate a discussion about what's happening in the picture, what kind of party it is, what kinds of food are shown, etc.

B. Match the questions and the answers.

1. Ask the questions orally as a comprehension check.

2. Have students read the questions and put the correct letter in the blank to answer.

3. Correct as a class.

Page 160

C. Look at the picture. Read the conversation and fill in the blanks.

1. Go over the directions. Explain that students will choose words from the box to write in the blanks.

2. Have students work independently.

3. Correct as a class.

4. Have students listen and repeat the lines of the dialogue.

5. Have class practice the dialogue in pairs.

Page 161 **I. Listening Comprehension***

    1. Go over the directions for Part I with students.

    2. Read each item of the script two times, at normal conversational speed.

        Script:
        1. It's an orange.

        2. They're carrots.

        3. Are these cucumbers?

        4. What kind of cookies would you like?

        5. Is it a dollar ninety–eight?

        6. How much are the peppers?

        7. What are those?

        8. What are these?

    *Cassette users can have students listen to the script on the tape.

Page 162 **II. Reading and III. Writing**

    1. Go over the directions for Parts II and III with students.

    2. Have class do these sections independently.

Evaluation check

    1. Correct evaluation by having student volunteers write their answers on the board or an overhead transparency.

    2. Have class check their answers.

    3. Circulate to make sure students have checked their work accurately.

Where Are the Children?

Communication Objectives:
>Identify places in the community
>Ask and answer questions about where people are

New Structures:
>Prepositions of place *at, by*
>Adverbs *here, there, over there*

Visuals:

V93	He's at the bank.
V94	She's at the market.
V95	They're at the post office.
V96	She's at the laundromat.
V97	She's at the beauty shop.
V98	He's at the drugstore.
V99	They're at the video store.
V100	He's at the barber shop.
V101	She's at the library.
V102	Let's Talk: Where Are the Children?
V19	a dishwasher (from Lesson 7)
V20	a waiter (from Lesson 7)
V29	students (from Lesson 8)
V31	teachers (from Lesson 8)
V103	Let's Talk: At the Library

Page 164 ✔ **Review:** A Party

>Plan a class party with refreshments and a shopping list.

Something New: Places in the Neighborhood

>1. Establish the context by talking about neighborhoods.

>2. Introduce the places in the neighborhood, using V93–101. Have students listen, then listen and repeat the vocabulary items, then full sentences.

Page 165 **Let's Talk:** Where Are the Children?*

>1. Show V102 to establish the context of the conversation: Sara and Tomas are just arriving home in the evening.

2. Model the dialogue as students listen, indicating the speakers by pointing to the visual or other means.

3. Model the dialogue again.

4. Model the dialogue and have class repeat.

5. Take one role and have class take other role; then change roles.

6. Divide class in half and have them take the two roles; then have them switch roles.

7. Have volunteers say the dialogue for the class.

 8. Have class open books and practice the dialogue in pairs.

*Cassette users can have students listen to the dialogue first with books closed.

Page 166 ☛ **Practice: "Where's Sara?"**

1. Cue with location visuals and persons.

> T: (Hold up visual V100) Bill.
> S1: Where's Bill?
> S2: He's at the barber shop.

2. Have students open their books and read the exercises.

■ Interaction: Where Am I?

Have students follow the procedure as stated in the lesson.

Page 167 ## Something New: Here and There

 1. Use your watch and the clock on the wall to establish concepts of *here* and *there*.

2. Show visuals of busser and waiter (V19–20), students and teachers (V29–30), from lessons 7 and 8 to show relationship of *here* and *there*.

3. Using the visuals, have students practice.

 4. Have students open their books and read the exercises.

Let's Talk: At the Library*

1. Show V103 to establish the context of the conversation.

2. Follow the procedure given in the Let's Talk section above for presenting the dialogue.

3. Have the students practice in pairs.

*Cassette users can have students listen to the dialogue first with books closed.

☛ Practices: "He's here" and "By the lemons"

1. Cue with illustrations and practice *here*, *there*, and *over there*. (Also use appropriate visuals from previous lessons: e.g., places in the neighborhood.)

2. Have students open their books and read the exercises.

■ **Interaction:** Where's Lisa?

Have students follow the procedure as stated in the lesson.

 Reading: My Neighborhood*

1. Establish context for Reading passage.

2. Have students read the passage independently.

3. Ask comprehension questions.

4. Have students read orally, as a class or in groups.

5. Have students discuss the story, using the discussion questions.

*Cassette users can have students listen to the Reading first with books closed.

✎ Writing

1. Have the students complete the exercises.

2. Go over the answers together.

Page 170 🔲 ***A. Listen and check the correct location.****

    1. Go over the directions and the places listed across the top of the grid.

    2. Play the tape or read the script for #1 and have students put a check mark under the video store for Tom. Continue with the remaining items.

Script:

1. A: Hi, can I speak to Tom?
   B: Sorry, he isn't here. He's at the video store.
   A: Where?
   B: The video store.
   A: Okay. Tell Tom, Sara called.

2. A: Hi, can I speak to Sara?
   B: Sorry she isn't here. She's at the market.
   A: Where?
   B: The market.
   A: Oh, tell Sara, Tony called.

3. A: Hi, is Tony there?
   B: No, he isn't. He's at the post office.
   A: He's where?
   B: At the post office.
   A: Please tell Tony, May called.

4. A: Good afternoon, is May there?
   B: No, she isn't. She's at the bank.
   A: She's where?
   B: At the bank.
   A: Please tell May, Richard called.

5. A: Hi, can I speak to Richard?
   B: He isn't here. He's at the library.
   A: Where?
   B: At the library.
   A: Oh. Please tell Richard, Maria called.

6. A: Hi, Maria?
   B: No, this is Sara. Maria's at the laundromat.
   A: Where is she?
   B: At the laundromat.
   A: Okay, please tell Maria, Tom called.

*Cassette users can have students listen to the script on tape.

3. Have students correct their work by comparing grids with other students or by marking answers on the board or a transparency of page 170.

B. Talk about Maria's appointment book with a partner.

 1. Go over the appointments shown in the book and the example questions. Ask a few questions to model.

 2. Have students ask and answer questions in pairs.

Page 171 **C. Now write questions and answers about Maria's appointment book.**

 1. Have students write the answers after the oral practice.

 2. Correct as a class by asking volunteers to read each item. Write items on the board if necessary.

Lesson 20

Where's My Wallet?

Communication Objectives:

Identify everyday items carried in pockets or handbags
Describe locations of items
Help someone find a lost item

New Structures:

Prepositions of place *in, on, under*

Visuals:

V104   a wallet
V105   a handbag/purse
V106   a pocket
V107   My identification cards are in my wallet
V108   Let's Talk: Where's My Wallet?

Other instructional aids:

Realia—Wallet
       Handbag
       ID Card
       Bills and coins

Page 172

✔ Review: Places in the Neighborhood

Have students use visuals V93–101 to practice questions with *where* and answers with *here* and *there*.

Something New: My Wallet

1. Present the objectives as stated in the lesson.

2. Establish context by discussing what we keep in our pockets and handbags.

3. Use visuals V104–106 or a wallet and actual items, and present the lesson.

4. Have students repeat the sentences after you.

Page 173

☞ Practice: "It's in my wallet"

1. Cue with illustrations or with realia and have students practice the prepositions of location according to where you place the items.

2. Have students open their books and read the exercises.

Page 174 **Let's Talk:** Where's My Wallet?*

1. Discuss break time activities.

2. Show V108 and establish the context.

3. Model the dialogue as students listen, indicating the speakers by pointing to the visual or other means.

4. Model the dialogue again.

5. Model the dialogue and have class repeat.

6. Take one role and have class take other role; then change roles.

7. Divide class in half and have them take the two roles; then have them switch roles.

8. Have volunteers say the dialogue for the class.

9. Have class open books and practice the dialogue in pairs.

*Cassette users can have students listen to the dialogue first with books closed.

Page 175 **☞ Practice: "Here it is"**

Cue with realia or illustrations and have students practice the exercises.

■ Interaction: Is It in the Purse?

Follow the procedures as stated in the lesson.

Reading: What's in the Bag?*

1. Establish context by using a handbag as a prop and identifying items in it.

2. Have students look at reading illustrations and read.

3. Have students carry on a discussion using the questions in the lesson.

*Cassette users can have students listen as they read and look at the illustration.

✍ **Writing**

Have students carry out the Writing assignment. Circulate to provide additional vocabulary as they make their lists.

☛ **Practice Activity: How many?**

 Have students use their lists to participate in the Activity.

Lesson 20 Activity Pages

A. Talk about the picture.

Lead a discussion about the items in the picture and their locations.

B. Look at the picture and write the missing words.

1. Read #1 as an example.

2. Have students continue.

3. Correct as a class.

C. Read and do it.

Explain that students will read instructions 1–5 and draw the items on the desk in the picture.

D. Look at the pictures. Listen to the conversation.*

1. Go over the order of the pictures. Explain that students will just listen to the story as they look at the pictures.

2. Play the tape or read the script at normal speed.

Script:
A: Oh no! Where are my keys?

B: They're over there, by your wallet.

A: No, those aren't my keys, those are quarters.

B: Oh, they're over there.

A: No, those are pens.

B: Ah yes. Your keys are there.

A: No, that's a lipstick. Ah–ha! Here they are.

B: Those aren't your keys!

A: Yes, they are! Ben, put on your glasses!

B: Oh no! Where are my glasses?

*Cassette users can have students listen to the script on tape.

Page 180 **E. Look at the pictures on page 179 and write the conversation.**
1. Go over the directions and the example.

2. Have students work independently to fill in the blanks.

3. Correct by reading and spelling the answers aloud.

4. Have students listen and repeat the lines of the dialogue.

5. Have students practice the dialogue in pairs.

F. Write three yes/no questions.
1. Explain the exercise and have students write questions individually or in pairs.

2. Check by circulating to offer help.

3. Have volunteers ask their questions for the whole class to answer.

Let's Cook Dinner!

Communication Objectives:
> Identify appliances and places in a kitchen
> Give and follow instructions
> Identify furniture in a living room

New Structures:
> Preposition of place *next to*

Visuals:
> V109 Rosa's Kitchen
> V110 Let's Talk: Let's Cook Dinner
> V111 Rosa's Living Room
> V70–77 Fruits (select from Lesson 16)
> V79–83 Vegetables (select from Lesson 17)

Page 182

✔ Review: What's in My Pocket?

Have students follow the directions as given in the lesson.

Something New: Rosa's Kitchen

1. Present the objectives as stated in the lesson.

2. Establish context by discussing kitchens and their functions.

3. Elicit statements about the students' kitchens.

4. Show V109 (on overhead, if possible) and identify the items in this kitchen.

Page 183

☞ Practice: "It's a stove"

1. Cue with V109 and ask students to identify the various items.

2. Have volunteers ask questions.

☞ Practice: "What are these?"

1. Follow the procedure for previous exercise.

2. Have students open their books and read the exercises.

■ Interaction: What's in Your Kitchen?

 Divide students into pairs or groups and have them discuss their own kitchens with each other.

Page 184 ## Let's Talk: Let's Cook Dinner!*

1. Discuss marketing. Who shops for food in your family? Where do you usually do your marketing?

2. Show visual V110 and establish context.

3. Model the dialogue as students listen, indicating the speakers by pointing to the visual or other means.

4. Model the dialogue again.

5. Model the dialogue and have class repeat.

6. Take one role and have class take other role; then change roles.

7. Divide class in half and have them take the two roles; then have them switch roles.

8. Have volunteers say the dialogue for the class.

 9. Have class open books and practice the dialogue in pairs.

*Cassette users can have students listen to the dialogue first with books closed.

☞ Practice: "It's on the counter"

 Have students use vegetable and fruit visuals from Lessons 16 and 17 as cues, and to make up locations for the answers.
          S1: Where's the cabbage?
          S2: It's on the counter.

☞ Practice: "They're next to the cabbage"

1. Follow the procedure for previous exercise.

 2. Have students open their books and read the exercises.

Page 185 ## ■ Interaction: Put the Carrots on the Counter

Follow the procedures as stated in the lesson.

▣ **Reading:** Rosa's Living Room*

1. Establish context by discussing living rooms and their functions.

2. Have students look at the illustration and name the furniture in the living room.

3. Have students read the passage independently.

4. Ask comprehension questions.

5. Have students read orally as a class or in groups.

6. Have students carry on a discussion using the questions.

*Cassette users can have students listen to the Reading on tape after step 3.

Page 186

✍ **Writing**

1. Have students complete the Writing.

2. Go over the answers with the class.

Lesson 21 Activity Page

Page 187

A. Read and answer the questions. Ask your partner the questions.

1. Go over the questions orally.

2. Have individuals read and write their answers.

3. Have pairs ask and answer the questions.

B. BINGO!

1. Go over the directions for the game and ask comprehension questions about what the students will do.

2. Practice the questions students will need to ask.

3. Have students walk around the room to ask the questions and write down the names of those who answer "yes."

4. Give a prize to the winner or winners.

Page 189 **I. Listening Comprehension***

    1. Go over the directions for Part I with students.

    2. Read each item of the script two times, at normal conversational speed.

        Script:
        1. He's at the post office.

        2. It's a beauty shop.

        3. They're over there.

        4. It's in the wallet.

        5. Please put the soda in the cabinet.

        6. The sofa is next to the TV.

    *Cassette users can have students listen to the script on the tape.

Page 190 **II. Reading and III. Writing**

    1. Go over the directions for Parts II and III with students.

    2. Have class do these sections independently.

Evaluation Check

    1. Correct evaluation by having student volunteers write their answers on the board or an overhead transparency.

    2. Have class check their answers.

    3. Circulate to make sure students have checked their work accurately.

Lesson 22

He's My Son

Communication Objectives:
> Identify terms for family members
> Talk about one's family to socialize

New Structures:
> Possessive *'s*
> Questions with *who*

Visuals:
> V112   The Kim Family
> V113   Don Kim, Jae Kim
> V114   Joe Kim, Lucy Kim
> V115   Mrs. Kim, Lucy
> V116   Mr. Kim, Joe
> V117   Let's Talk: He's My Son

Page 192

✔ Review: In, On, Under

Have pairs ask each other about locations of common objects they usually have with them.

Something New: The Kim Family

1. Briefly give the objectives of the lesson.

2. Show V112 of Mr. and Mrs. Kim and the three children and tell class that it is a family: the parents and children.

3. Using visuals V113–116, go into each type of relationship: husband and wife, son, daughter, sister, brother.

4. Check for comprehension of vocabulary.

Page 193

☞ Practice: "Who is he?"

1. Ask, "Who's he/she?" and "Who are they?" with each of the visuals in turn.

2. Have class open books and read what they have been practicing orally (pages 193–194) in pairs.

Page 195 **Let's Talk:** He's My Son*

1. Show V117 to establish the context: Friends talking about their families, showing off family photos.

2. Model the dialogue as students listen, indicating the speakers by pointing to the visual or other means.

3. Model the dialogue again.

4. Model the dialogue and have class repeat.

5. Take one role and have class take other role; then change roles.

6. Divide class in half and have them take the two roles; then have them switch roles.

7. Have volunteers say the dialogue for the class.

8. Have class open books and practice the dialogue in pairs.

*Cassette users can have students listen to the dialogue first with books closed.

☛ **Practice: "He's Jae's husband"**

1. Use visuals to practice structure points: Who…? and the possessive nouns: Mrs. Kim's son/daughter/husband.

2. Have class open books and read Practice (pages 195–196) in pairs.

Page 197 ☛ **Practice Activity: Introduce the Kim family**

1. Have five students roleplay members of the Kim family.

2. Ask one of the five students to introduce members of his "family" to the class. (This is my family: My mother, father, etc.)

3. Have another student from the class introduce the family, using one of the members as his friend: e.g., This is my friend Lucy's family: Lucy's parents, brothers, etc.

 Reading: Saturday Morning*

1. Have class look at the illustration and identify the people in the picture and where they are in the home.

2. Have class read the story independently.

Delta's Apple Pie, Teacher's Guide 1A

3. Go over the discussion questions in the usual way.

*Cassette users can have students listen to the Reading after looking at the illustration.

Page 198

✍ Writing

Have students do the Writing in usual way. Correct as a class.

Page 199

★ Something Extra: My Family

1. Have students draw members of their family and write their names below the pictures.

 2. Then in pairs or small groups have them tell who the members of their family are to the others in the group.

3. Have them write a story to introduce the people in the picture to the reader. (This part can be saved for an extra activity as students finish the regular Writing activity.)

Extension Activity: Family Photographs or Snapshots

Ask students to bring photographs of members of their family to share with other students. You can use the photos for the Review on page 202.
[Note: You may want to show a photo of your own family as a model for this activity.]

Page 200 **A. Listen and name the family members.***

    1. Explain that students will copy each name next to the correct person as they listen at normal speed.

    2. Play the tape or read the script at normal speed. Repeat the whole script if necessary.

> **Script:**
> This is the Gonzalez family. The father's name is Hector.
>
> His wife's name is Vera.
>
> Hector and Vera have two children.
>
> Their daughter's name is Betty.
>
> Their son's name is Chris.
>
> Betty and Chris are sister and brother.
>
> They are the children.
>
> Hector and Vera are their parents.

    *Cassette users can have students listen to the script on tape.

    3. Check answers by asking questions about the family.

B. Look at the picture. Read the answers and write the questions.

    1. Go over the directions and the example.

    2. Have the students work independently.

    3. Correct by having volunteers say the questions and then write them of the board. Check the questions on the board together.

    4. Have students compare their questions to those on the board. Circulate to make sure students are checking their work accurately.

Page 201 **C. Look at the picture and write the missing words in the story.**

    1. Go over the directions and have students work independently.

    2. Read the story aloud to check their answers.

We're Cousins

Communication Objectives:
> Identify terms for extended family members
> Ask if people are related to socialize

New Structures:
> Predicate adjective *related*

Visuals:
> V118 Jim Garcia and his family
> V119 Victor Garcia and his family
> V120 Let's Talk: We're Cousins

Page 202

✔ Review: Family

1. Have pairs or groups talk about the Kim family, then about their own families.

2. Optional Activity, if assigned from previous day: Ask volunteers to show photos and tell the class about their families. Have the class ask and answer questions about their families.

Something New: More Family Members

1. Briefly state the objectives of the lesson.

2. Use V118 to introduce Jim Garcia and his wife, son, and daughter.

3. Now use V119 to introduce Jim's brother Victor, Victor's wife Sonia, and Victor's daughters Luisa and Cecilia.

4. Explain the relationships: Victor to Peter and Gina, Jim to Luisa and Cecilia.

5. Explain Luisa and Cecilia's relationship to Peter and Gina.

6. Check comprehension by asking yes/no and either/or questions.

7. Have class repeat relationships, then answer questions about the family.

☞ **Practice: "He's Luisa's uncle"**

 Go over the Practice questions after oral practice; have class open their books and read in pairs.

  Let's Talk: We're Cousins*

1. Show V120 to establish the context of the conversation: Mrs. Baker is talking to two students in her class.

2. Model the dialogue as students listen, indicating the speakers by pointing to the illustration or other means.

3. Model the dialogue again.

4. Model the dialogue and have class repeat.

5. Take one role and have class take other role; then change roles.

6. Divide class in half and have them take the two roles; then have them switch roles.

7. Have volunteers say the dialogue for the class.

 8. Have class open books and practice the dialogue in pairs.

*Cassette users can have students listen to the dialogue first with books closed.

☞ **Practices: "Are you related?" and "He's my uncle"**

1. Go over the Practice items in the book.

2. Practice the structure "Are you _____ ?" and "Are you and Joe _____ ?" questions, making sure students understand that "you" is plural and is answered with the plural pronoun "we."

3. Have students read the practice conversations in pairs, referring back to the pictures of the two families on page 202 if necessary.

Extension Activity: Family Chart

1. Go back to the visuals V118–119 showing Jim and Victor Garcia's families.

2. Make a chart showing each family member and connecting Jim and Victor in a "family tree."

Maria—Jim—brothers—Victor—Sonia
Gina—Peter—cousins—Luisa—Cecilia

3. Next to Jim and Victor, show that they are brothers.

4. Next to the children, show that they are cousins.

5. Go over the chart, asking and answering discussion questions:

      a. Who are brothers?
      b. Who are sister and brother?
      c. Who are sisters?
      d. Who are cousins?

6. Have students make a chart of their families, showing their parents and their brothers and sisters. Have them show an uncle or an aunt (one is all that is needed) with the uncle/aunt's children. Have them indicate the names of their cousins.

Page 205 ■ **Interaction:** Talk about Families

Have students talk in small groups about their extended families: the number of aunts and uncles on their mother's side, and then on their father's side of the family; then the number of cousins that they have.

Page 206 🔊 **Reading:** The Kim Family*

1. Have students read independently.

2. Have them read again and draw pictures for Practice Activity #1 (Don's brothers and sisters) and Practice Activity #2 (Don's children) using stick figures or "happy" faces.

3. Go over the number of people, names, ages, etc. that should be in the pictures to check comprehension.

4. Have students do Practice Activity #3; then share it and talk about it with a partner.

*Cassette users can have students listen to the Reading first with books closed.

Page 207 ✍ **Writing**

1. Have students fill in answers in the usual way.
[Note: You might review who's who in the two families before they begin.]

2. Correct as a class.

Page 208

A. Put the words in pairs. Write the words for men on the left. Write the words for women on the right.

    1. Go over the examples.

    2. Have pairs or individuals categorize the words.

    3. Correct by having volunteers write the words in two columns on the board or a transparency.

B. Look at the family tree and answer the questions.

    1. Go over the directions and review the family trees. Remind the class that Jim and Victor are brothers, so their families are related.

    2. Have students read the questions independently and write single–word answers in the blanks.

    3. Correct as a class.

He's at Work

Communication Objectives:
>
> Answer the telephone
>
> Ask for someone on the telephone
>
> Explain that someone is *at work* or *at school*

New Structures:
>
> *This is...* to identify oneself on the phone
>
> Prepositional phrases with *at*
>
> Questions with *where*

Visuals:

V18	nurse (from Lesson 7)
V21	cook (from Lesson 7)
V121	He's at home.
V122	They're at school.
V123	Let's Talk: Is Your Husband at Home?

Page 210

✔ Review: Are You Related?

1. Elicit from class the names of students with the same last names. Write these names on the board.

2. Draw the interactive grid from the book on the board, filling in the names of the people with the same last names.

3. Have class ask if these people are related. "Are you related?" If people are related, they need to fill in the nature of the relationship (cousins, brothers, husband and wife, etc.).

Page 211

Something New: At Work and At Home

1. Use visuals V21, V121, and V122 to present new phrases: at work, at home, at school.

2. Ask yes/no and either/or questions, then "Where" questions to check comprehension.

3. Have class listen and repeat sentences.

Let's Talk: Is Your Husband at Home?*

1. Show V123 to establish the context of the conversation: Asking for someone on the phone.

2. Model the dialogue as students listen, indicating the speakers by pointing to the visual or other means.

3. Model the dialogue again.

4. Model the dialogue and have class repeat.

5. Take one role and have class take other role; then change roles.

6. Divide class in half and have them take the two roles; then have them switch roles.

7. Have volunteers say the dialogue for the class.

 8. Have class open books and practice the dialogue in pairs.

*Cassette users can have students listen to the dialogue first with books closed.

Page 212 ☛ **Practice: "This is Mrs. Kim"**

 1. Give students opportunity to answer a telephone and identify themselves on the phone by using the term "This is…."

2. Form practice drill for various situations: The call being for the person answering, the call for someone who is at home, as well as for a person who is not at home.

3. Practice the general responses "at home," "at school," and "at work" to the question "Where…?"

 4. Have students open books to practice both exercises.

Page 213 **Let's Review:** At Work and At Home

 1. Show V18, V121 and V122 as you tell each story. Ask comprehension questions about each one.

 2. Have students open books to read the three passages independently.

3. Then have students read and do the Practice "She's at work" (#1–5) in pairs.

■ Interaction: At Home, School, and Work

1. Practice the questions that students are going to ask each other as a class before they divide into groups.

2. After Interaction, ask volunteers to report back on what they have learned about their group members' families.

🔲 Reading: On the Telephone*

1. Explain that Paul is Ana's college–age son. He is away at school in another city. He's calling his mother on the phone.

2. Have students read independently.

3. Ask discussion questions.

*Cassette users can have students listen to the Reading first with books closed.

✍ Writing

1. Have class do Writing.

2. Correct as a class.

Lesson 24 Activity Pages

A. Talk about the pictures.

Lead a discussion about Mrs. Lee, Mr. Lee, Sally and Sam, and where they are in the pictures. Have students give you as much information as they can about the pictures.

B. Look at the pictures and write the answers to the questions.

1. Go over the directions and the example.

2. Have students work independently.

3. Correct answers orally and/or by having volunteers write them on the board or on a transparency of page 216.

4. Optional: Have pairs ask each other the questions.

C. Write your information and then ask your partner.

1. Have individuals write their answers to the questions.

2. Have pairs ask and answer the questions.

Unit Eight Evaluation

Page 219 **I. Listening Comprehension***

1. Go over the directions for Part I with students.

2. Read each item of the script two times, at normal conversational speed.

Script:
1. He's the husband

2. She's the mother.

3. They're cousins.

4. They're parents.

5. They're brothers.

6. She's at home.

7. Where is she?

8. Where are they?

*Cassette users can have students listen to the script on the tape.

Page 220 **II. Reading and III. Writing**

1. Go over the directions for Parts II and III with students.

2. Have class do these sections independently.

Evaluation Check

1. Correct evaluation by having student volunteers write their answers on the board or an overhead transparency.

2. Have class check their answers.

3. Circulate to make sure students have checked their work accurately.

Notes

Notes